The Book of the Bitterbump

The Folk-history of Cheshire's Wildlife

by
Roger Stephens © 2003

with illustrations by the author

Published by Gordon Emery
27 Gladstone Road, Chester CH1 4BZ
01244 377955

Printed by Masons Print Group   01244 674433

To the
CHESHIRE WILDLIFE TRUST
in celebration of its fortieth anniversary.

Contents

Opposite: It alighted on one of the turrets on the Town Hall (see page 67).

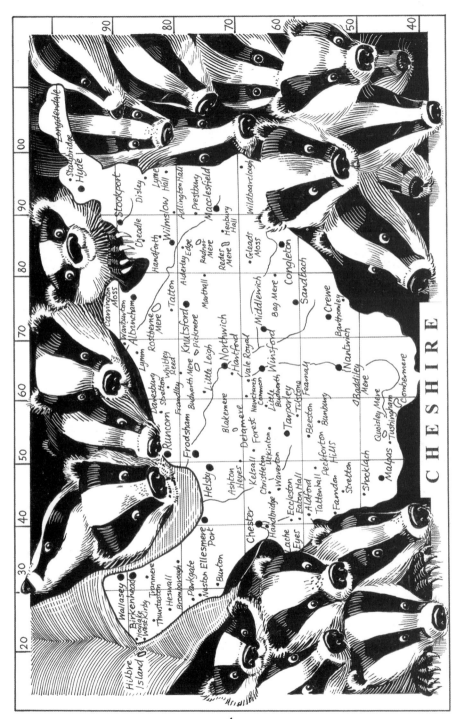

CHESHIRE

If a peewit nests on a bank, we can expect a rainy spell.

Foreword

The idea for this book came to me one cruelly cold March day at Frodsham marshes, while birdwatching with a few friends. A mixed flock of peewit and golden plover was feeding on the marsh and my companions, all good ornithologists, talked about the peewit's life-cycle, migration and feeding habits as we watched. By the end of the day, I had learned a good deal just by listening to them. As we wandered home, however, we got chatting to a man who had lived in the area all his life. He knew things that none of us knew: that the peewit has the local name *lappinch*; that he and his contemporaries used to collect their eggs to eat; that marshland was once known in Cheshire as *peewit land*; that if one of these birds nests on a bank we can expect a rainy spell. It struck me that these two kinds of knowledge - one scientifically correct, but lacking local roots, the other marred by superstition but growing out of our own history - had much to teach one another. I decided to collect more of this knowledge and write a folk-history of Cheshire's wildlife.

Such an approach has an honourable history in Cheshire, particularly in the writings of one of our finest naturalists, Arnold Boyd. He knew that the study of wild creatures is greatly enriched when it includes the people who know them best: the local farmers, labourers, gamekeepers and poachers, with all their experience, lore and knowledge.

But books like *A Country Parish* and *The Country Diary of a Cheshire Man* are now more than half a century out of date. I felt it was time to continue his work. At first, I was full of doubts. Would anybody still remember the old country lore and, even if they did, would they tell me? Back in 1883, the Frodsham folklorist Robert Holland had that sort of problem: *"Our peasantry...are, as a rule, a little reticent about such matters..."* His questions often received those baffling replies (e.g. *"Down Wettenhall Lane, the plovers fly backwards"*) that the countryman uses to put off nosey outsiders. Would I do any better, 120 years on?

I spent many happy days in my local reference library, poring over old magazines, newspapers and books to unfold the story of Cheshire's fauna and its changing fortunes over the centuries and wrote magazine articles requesting contributions from readers. Over the months, my files of research grew fatter and fatter and, before long, letters were dropping onto the mat. They came from all corners of the county, mostly from old folk, eager to pass on their wildlife anecdotes and the superstitions and dialect names they knew. It was their enthusiasm that finally convinced me that the book needed to be written. Then came the most enjoyable part of the job: cycling out on bright-skied mornings to meet some of them. What a simple joy it is to sit at a cottage fireside, supping tea and being entrusted with precious gems from an old person's memory! Then, home again through familiar, twisting lanes, mulling over what I had learned as the shadows lengthened and bats began to flutter silently overhead. Although the amount of fieldwork here is quite small (just *scratching the iceberg* as one of my contacts put it), I learned enough to confirm that a surprising amount of the nature lore noted by Boyd and others is still with us today and there is also much which escaped their notice.

So, if you love wildlife, know Cheshire and want to rediscover what your great grandparents knew, this book is for you. Wherever possible, I have stood aside to let Cheshire people, living and dead, tell the story themselves, which is why, on first leafing through this book, you may have thought it overburdened with quotations. I must not forget to acknowledge the living ones who contributed to it, in particular, Tom Allen, Kenneth Ball, Freda Bloomer, Alan Booth, Tom Edmondson, Graham Fergus, Eric Gandy, Eric Hardy, Graham Harrison, Len Johnson, Jim Jones, Lynn Lees, Avril Lewis, John Lloyd, Norman Mursell, Hazel Pryor, Marietta Richardson, May Rosedale, Martin Stead, Pat Walton, Len Witter and R.S. Wynne. Thanks also to Tony Bowerman, Gordon Emery, Joan Fairhurst, Nick mcGrinn, Ian Smith, Karen Taylor and Steve Woolfall for help and encouragement and to Marie Passingham and Terry Walsh, for posing whilst I drew them!

A couple more points need clarifying. Firstly, some of the people that I talked to used local words and expressions which I have seen no reason not to include in the text. There is a Glossary at the back of the book, which will surprise those who imagine that Cheshire people speak no dialect. Secondly, when I say *Cheshire*, I mean the great county that stood for 900 years (see the map on page four), not the ever-changing modern version. Now read on...

6

I can't remember hearing a cuckoo sing from Hartford's cuckoo tree.

Chapter 1

The Cuckoo Tree

"1688: April, snowed 3 days. The cucco did sing before hathorns were greene."

from a memorandum book of John Ryle of High Greave, Cheadle.

When I was a child, all the best trees for climbing and conkering had names, names we learned from older kids who, of course, had done the same when they were younger. But one tree, a tall, dead one, had a name I didn't understand: the Cuckoo Tree. In its prime, it must have been a local landmark but, by my day, it was just a gaunt, leafless skeleton. Why was it called the Cuckoo Tree? That question never troubled me as a boy but, thirty years later, it popped up in my head and I appealed for information through the local press. The answer came promptly enough, from the local naturalist and writer, Eric Hardy. This, he explained, was the tree where local people would listen out for the first cuckoo each spring, hoping to be the first to hear it and so enjoy good luck for the rest of the year. But can the bird really find its way to the traditional tree year after year? According to many bird-watchers, yes, and often on a traditional day (in Cheshire, April 15th). To receive the good luck, you have to be abroad early and have coins in your pocket, ready to turn them over as you hear the sound. An old Eaton estate worker from

Aldford once told me that there used to be great rivalry among the labourers to be the first to hear the first cuckoo as he approached along Aldford Brook. They called him *The Welsh Ambassador* since, like most of our summer visitors, he enters the county from the west, giving Cestrians the good luck a day or two before Maxonians.

It's difficult, nowadays, to picture the impact that the cuckoos' arrival had in the days when they were common. Geoffrey Egerton-Warburton, in his book *In a Cheshire Garden* (1912), wrote: *"The coming of the cuckoo seems to be of more interest to people here* [the village of Warburton, near Lymm] *than any event in natural history, and cuckoos are, I should say, more plentiful with us than in many places, and are nearly as often seen as heard. I must have seen a dozen one day in May from the high road during a short drive of a few miles, and, generally speaking, in May not a day (I should not be far out if I said not an hour of the day) goes by without our knowing by sight as well as sound that there are cuckoos in the garden".* Hence the old Cheshire saying: *As hoarse as a cuckoo !* In Egerton-Warburton's day, almost every village must once have had its own cuckoo tree, but they are hard to find on the map: Cranage has a field called *Cuckoo Oak*, Gawsworth a *Cuckoo Thorn,* and there are a few *Cuckoo Fields* and *Cuckoo Lanes,* but not much more. Only the oral historian, it seems, can hope to find cuckoo trees.

In the days when bird migration was poorly understood, the cuckoo's disappearance in August must have been just as puzzling. One of my classmates at Hartford Primary School told me that it spent the colder months as a sparrowhawk, turning back into a cuckoo in spring and, looking through Boyd's *Country Diary,* I see the same thing was believed in the 1930s: *"A local poacher, an observant man who knows a lot about birds, once asked me if I realised that they made this startling change. When I asked for proof he replied, 'Well, there's the field', and clearly thought such evidence proof enough for anybody. I had to agree that the field certainly was there, and we left it at that."*

A newly-fledged cuckoo, can look uncannily like a sparrowhawk and may even have evolved this disguise as a protection during the vulnerable weeks before it begins its long, unaided migration to Africa. Unfortunately, it had the opposite effect on gamekeepers, who used to shoot cuckoos before they had a chance to metamorphose.

There are strange beliefs surrounding the female cuckoo's bubbling note, also. In some parts of Cheshire, it was thought that the fledgling made this sound as it devoured its foster-parent while, in other areas, they thought it was sucking the other eggs, as in this Cheshire version of the well-known folk song:

> The cuckoo is a pretty bird, he calls as he flies,
> He brings us good tidings and tells us no lies.
> He takes other birds' eggs to make his voice clear,
> And he calls "cuckoo" three months of the year.

The *good tidings*, of course, means the promise of summer and that, I suppose, explains the good luck as well. But is that all there is to it? Boyd found evidence of a more practical, agricultural reason for hearing the first cuckoo. Before the days of weather forecasts, farmers looked to the natural world for guidance on when to sow and reap their crops. Oats, for example, were once by far the most important cereal in Cheshire, grown to feed both horses and people. But the sowing of oats was a ticklish matter. Put them in too early and the seedlings might get backened by a cold snap; too late and they would still be *fast at one end* in late August, when a *dumberdash* might *croodle them down* and ruin the entire crop. Thus, in the absence of meteorological help, the first shout of the cuckoo, a sound already saturated in folklore, was taken as the signal that all oats should now have been planted. Any sown after this time were called *'cuckoo-wuts'* and their prospects written off. As an old Cheshire saying puts it: *Cuckoo wuts and woodcock hay, make the farmer run away.* Boyd noted this example from his own district (Frandley): *"A farmer was seriously worried by the early arrival of the cuckoo, and asked anxiously how far distant was the bird I had just heard and seen. He was greatly relieved to hear that it was almost two miles away and nowhere within earshot of the field in which he still had to sow his oats... There was no more delay; the field was sown immediately and the farmer's mind set at rest."* (Country Diary, 20/4/1944). A similar stigma was attached to lambs that were born late: *cuckoo-lambs* were not expected to live long.

The planting of other crops was signalled by other birds. The yellow wagtail, which reaches us at about the same time as the cuckoo (and used to be one of its favourite foster parents) prompted the farmer to plant his potatoes. Cheshire's great tradition of tater-growing dates back to the Napoleonic wars when fears of hunger led to widespread planting and, even today, they are among the best grown anywhere. Yellow wagtails like to raise their young in potato fields, where the large, floppy leaves hide the nest from predators. Like the cuckoos, they like to return to their roots, and yearling birds are thought to drop into the very fields where they were raised, just as the next crop is being set. This association has earned it the folk-names *potato-dropper* and *tater-setter* (in other parts of the country it is the *barley bird* or the *oaseed bird*). Boyd again: *"On April 11th my first yellow wagtail of the year rose from under the heels of the mare as she grazed in the paddock. It then flew straight across three fields and settled on one of the potato drills worked by a neighbouring farmer, who took it as a good sign, for he was taught as a boy to call this bird a 'potato-setter' and to take its arrival as a sign to begin. Within three miles other more daring farmers have potato plants already well above ground, and the night frosts of this week have cost them dear."* (16/4/1938)

Like cuckoos, these summer visitors were supposed to spend the winter as another species, in this case, the closely-related grey wagtail. Until recently, large gatherings of yellow wagtails were a common sight, not just in potato fields but in marshy pastures and damp meadows where the brilliant plumage of the males outshone the newly-opened kingcups. Guy Farrar, one of Cheshire's best bird-writers called them *"the golden harbingers of spring"*. They fed among the cattle, waiting for insects to be disturbed, then catching them on the wing with aerobatic panache. A 1950 monograph on the

9

species declared that Cheshire was *"the county for the yellow wagtail"* and noted that they seemed to be increasing. So where are they now? We still have plenty of potato fields, but nowadays they contain little more than well-sprayed potato plants. The golden harbingers of spring can still be spotted on mizzicky ground along the Gowy, Dee and Mersey valleys, but now they must be sought out with a good pair of binoculars. A succession of droughts in the Sahara desert may have made migration more perilous for them.

In the back-end, when the potatoes had all been got and the summer visitors have vanished from the fields, farmers have to think about planting winter wheat. Now there are new invaders winging in from the north; squadrons of chattering fieldfares and redwings flashing across the wintry sky. These Vikings are bred in the forests of Scandinavia and, after a long sea-crossing, make their way overland from east to west, pillaging the hedgerows as they go. The first raiders reach Cheshire towards the end of October, to be followed by the main army in November. These birds are the third traditional planting signal, as Boyd again tells us: *"There has been some delay in ploughing for winter wheat; a farmer told me he was glad he had not seen any "bluebacks" (fieldfares) yet, as he always reckoned to finish sowing his wheat before they came."* (4/11/1943) However, this may not be just another superstition, as a farmer's daughter from Ashton Hayes explained to me. Her father was equally anxious to get his wheat sown before the bluebacks appeared, but with good reason - he knew that, if he delayed, the huge flocks would descend on his fields and eat up all the seed!

In the case of the promiscuous, cuckolding cuckoo, however, there is little doubt that its connection with seed-sowing is due to ancient notions of fertility. While he sings, his erect pintle, or cuckoo pint, pops up in the hedgebanks and his frothy love-juice is skittered over the grass (today we call it *cuckoo spit*, but our forefathers used a ruder name). Is this why the oat seeds must be in the soil, awaiting its arrival?

So, do you have a local cuckoo tree? If so, when did you last hear a cuckoo shout from it? Like yellow wagtails, they are now spread much more thinly, so many of those forgotten cuckoo trees must stand idle every April. As Lenna Bickerton, of Lostock Gralam, wrote in her *Memories of a Cheshire Childhood: "The cuckoo visited us bang on time in early spring, and from then on his plaintive call could be heard for the rest of the spring and summer until his voice became croaked and muffled and he was ready to fly away. As the oaks and hedgerows have disappeared, so has he."*

Now that I think of it, I can't remember hearing a cuckoo sing from Hartford's cuckoo tree. Those fields are lost under houses now and, in any case, the residents have no time to listen out for bird calls as they drive off to work every morning.

Oddly enough, otters had some friends among the fishermen.

Chapter 2

What *is* a Bitterbump?

And what, for that matter, is a *glead,* a *daker hen*, or a *lich fowl*? They are all local names for creatures that were once a familiar part of the Cheshire countryside but are now all but forgotten. Yet, we should treasure these dialect names, for they, along with old sayings and place-names, are often the best evidence we have. The word *bitterbump*, for example, is found in Bridge's *Old Cheshire Proverbs* (1917); someone with big feet was told: *"Thou'rt like a bitterbump; thy foot's longer than thy leg"*. Coward and Oldham, when researching their *Fauna of Cheshire* (1910), found old folk all over the county whose parents remembered its booming call echoing around the Cheshire meres at dusk and dawn. Boyd (born 1885) was just old enough to remember it at Whitley Reed, one of the great wildernesses of Cheshire before reclamation and enclosure began in the 1850s. It was a strange sound, deep and resonant, yet oddly muffled like a distant foghorn, and audible up to three miles away. Some believed that it plunged its face deep into the slutch as it sang to create this effect. In fact, the male bitterbump jangles his neck muscles with a violent blast of air to make this haunting noise.

The bitterbump, if you have not already guessed, is that most secretive of birds: the bittern. Only a handful of pairs now nest in Britain - none of them in our county - and they are near the top of every *twitcher's* list of wanted birds. You may find it hard to believe that there was ever a time when the boom of a bittern created no more excitement than the skrike of a moorhen, but such is the case. Listen to Reverend John Pickford, writing in 1882: *"Well do I remember some thirty-five years ago going on a piscatorial expedition to Bagmere, and after a long fatiguing walk on a glorious July day, such as we used formerly to have in England, finding it impossible to get at the pool. A broad belt of sedges and rushes and marshy ground rendered access impracticable...There was a weird aspect about the place, and the silence was broken by the boom of the bittern and the call of the moorhen."* (Quoted in *Cheshire Notes and Queries*, 1900).

It's just as difficult to picture the great whispering wildernesses of fen that once existed in Cheshire. Such places were called *butland* by the old Cheshire farmers (i.e. land fit only for bitterbumps), much as their modern counterparts refer to marsh as *peewit land*. Unlike its cousin the grey heron, the bittern needs watery reedbeds big enough to lose itself in if it is to raise a brood. Today, such places - lonely, misty, smelly places - have been all but cleansed from the Cheshire plain. So, is that boom a sound lost forever, like the howl of the wolf and the slap of a beaver's tail? Not quite. A Chester man tells me that, when fishing on the canal near Mollington, in the 1960s, he used to hear it every summer, coming from secluded fishponds nearby. Even today, the occasional storm-blown stray finds shelter at Rostherne or Budworth Mere, and there have been reports of booming males. A nestful of baby bitterbumps in Cheshire is still only a dream for us, but it's a dream worth dreaming. Perhaps, if we all keep the boom of the bitterbump echoing in our hearts; it will have a chance of returning for real.

The name *glead* has ancient roots but, like the shrill mewing of the bird itself, it is rarely heard in modern Cheshire. It can be found on the map, however: Gleadsmoss, near Withington, marks one of its old homes, as does Gleadshill Cob, in Delamere Forest. The name tells us something about its flight, since it comes from the Old English *glida* - literally, *"the glider"*. Today, we call it the red kite. Once, it was a ubiquitous scavenger in both town and country, cleaning mess from the streets, though it was also *"wont to snatch the food out of the children's hands"* (William Turner, 1540). During the Middle Ages, it was given legal protection for its services to sanitation but, by Tudor times, its nuisance value was deemed to outweigh its usefulness and so the killing began. In 1656, Daniel King was able to record, in his *Vale Royal*, that gleads were still common in the forests of Delamere and Macclesfield, but they already had a bounty on their heads. Like jays and carrion crows, they survived by hiding themselves away in game coverts and other small woodlands. There is a testimony to this in a letter by Lord Stanley of Alderley (dated 1791), in which he describes a moving visit to his birthplace: *"Here was I returned to the same spot where life had begun. On the other side of this mere [Radnor] the eye rests on a thick, venerable wood of beech trees above 140 years old, planted by one of our great-grandfathers on his marriage. There are no trees so large in the country... The finest gloom is caused by the blended branches of the woods, and the silence that reigns there is only broken by the shrieks of the large kites, which constantly build their nests in the neighbourhood, and the calls of the teal and the wild ducks to each other in the mere."* By the end of the 19th century, red kites had only one home in all Britain: a remote valley in Wales, where four or five nests could still be found. It has taken another century and a lot of hard conservation work to coax their numbers up to today's stable population. Today, kites are occasionally seen gliding over their ancient haunts in Cheshire and even over the city of Chester, so keep a tight hold on your butties!

A similar effort will be needed to rescue the black grouse, a bird that was once as familiar on farmland as the partridge and the pheasant but now subsists on the scrubby margins of moorland. In *The Old Brown Forest*, one of Warburton's famous Hunting Songs (1837), there is a reference to black grouse in the *Forest of Mara (Delamere):*

> *"There, where the flock on sweet herbage once fed,*
> *The blackcock takes wing, and the fox-cub is bred."*

This is not poetic licence, for we know that black grouse were regularly shot in those parts at least until the 1860s, when the wife of Thomas Linnell, forester of Delamere, recalled, in a letter: *"There was a good supply of black game, pheasants, partridges, hares and rabbits, but when the railway was being made between Manchester and Chester, the game disappeared".* They also bred on other wooded heaths such as Rudheath where, as they roosted, poachers shot them by torchlight. By the end of the century, black grouse had quietly slipped away from the plain.

In 1901, Lord Delamere released birds on Newchurch Common and Abbots Moss, hoping to re-establish them, but only provided fast food for foxes. By this time, only one corner of Cheshire still echoed to the sneezing and *rookooing* calls of blackcocks: the clough woods of the Dane and Goyt valleys. Here one could still witness *lekking* - the unique, magnificent, absurd, unforgettable mating display of the male birds. But even here, rushy meadows were being drained and sheep were multiplying into a voracious army. By the early 1960s, the black grouse had been starved out and have rarely been seen in the county since.

Our heaths and mosses have fared even worse than the moorlands. In their heyday, they supported a wonderful variety of moths, which attracted not only lepidopterists but a mysterious insectivore known, in some parts of the county, as a *moth owl*: the nightjar. In Wirral, it was *"an abundant summer visitor to the firwoods of Bidston, Storeton, Ness and Burton, also to the open heath of Bidston Hill"* (J.F. Brockholes, *Birds of Wirral*, 1874). This reminiscence of Wirral by folklorist Fletcher Moss sets the scene: *"Even in the twilight there was plenty to see, to hear, or to think about. There was a strange charm in those gorse-clad hills, where willow-wrens or other little warblers warbled from every bush, where the cuckoos called across the water to the cuckoos of Wales, and as the darkness deepened those ghostly birds the nightjars jarred or churred their gently rattling grumbles all around..."* Before the Second World War, one could walk for a

13

couple of miles through Delamere forest as dusk came on and hear the distinctive churring sound from four or five different birds. It was equally well-known throughout the Mid-Cheshire ridge, the eastern hills and on the mosses and heaths of the plain.

The sound could even be a mither, as a Helsby woman wrote to tell me: *"...My mother used to tell me that, as a girl living at the foot of Helsby Hill in the early part of the last century, 1900 to 1915 approximately, she was kept awake at night by the nightjars on the hill. We once had masses of bilberries there but no longer..."* We can blame the encroaching trees for both those losses: the nightjars and the bilberries. My most recent records all come from the late fifties: several people remember nightjars at Hatchmere around that time. A Frodsham man remembers watching them fly over a young conifer plantation, clapping their long, hawk-like wings as they twisted and turned in pursuit of moths and dragonflies. An acquaintance of his found a nest and photographed it as proof of breeding. These must have been among the very last for, by 1958, they had vanished.

Norman Ellison, the BBC naturalist who lived in West Kirby, wrote of hearing nightjars near his home during the same decade. On soft, summer evenings the continuous, two-note reeling would lure him out in his slippers to a copse of turkey oaks on Caldy Hill where the singer was hidden. But he was enjoying such experiences less and less often, due, he thought, to disturbance by dog-walkers. By that time, our climate had swung towards cool springs and damp summers, a trend which has made life hard for the nightjar and other summer migrants, like the wryneck. The last nightjar nest to be seen in Wirral was at Frankby in June 1973. Conservation bodies are now managing the remaining fragments of our heathland so that this bird will find a home if it ever chooses to return.

Another characteristic sound of balmy summer evenings long ago was the rasping voice of the daker hen, land rail or corncrake. Coward believed it to be commoner in Cheshire than in any county to the south: *"During the last week in April or the first few days of May the familiar call of the Land Rail...may be heard in the lowlands and on the hill-pastures up to the edge of the moors...during May, June and July, its presence is advertised day and night by its monotonous and incessant 'crake'"*. Like the nightjar, it was a very effective *'knocker-up'*, wakening sleepers too early and nagging them till they got up. According to Moss, people could be driven to desperate measures: *"I saw several men calling corncrakes to shoot them, for one of them said he was kept awake at night by their nois."*. (*Chronicles of Cheadle*, 1894).

Many were shot accidentally in September, when partridge shooting began; they would be flushed out of cover along with the gamebirds. Or was it accidental? Some say that, due to food shortages during the 1914-18 war, many corncrakes ended up in the pot. I doubted this until I looked into Mrs. Beeton's legendary *Book of Household Management* (1861) and found a recipe for roast corncrake!

This summer visitor was recorded in the papers as a welcome sign of spring, like the cuckoo today: *"On Friday the corncrake was 'creaking' in a meadow between Shotwick*

14

and Saughall village..."(Chester Chronicle 19/5/1917) and, just as the cuckoo was supposed to turn into a hawk for the winter, the corncrake was thought to grow a long, red beak and become a water rail! Many Cheshire farmers believed that a good year for corncrakes foretold an equally good hay crop. Everyone knew the sound but, as it spent the whole summer hidden in the cool green of hay meadows, it was rarely seen. Following its call was no good either, for between each pair of raucous notes it legged it to another part of the field, so quickly that many credited it with ventriloquial abilities. Harry Neilson, claimed, in his book *Auld Lang Syne* (1935), to have been one of the lucky ones: *"Fern owls or nightjars bred in the woods yearly near Club House* [Bidston], *while I have often watched the elusive corncrake mother, conducting her brood of tiny chicks to safety in corn and grass field"*. Several of my elderly correspondents mentioned hearing the call when they were children, like this Wallasey man: *"Your interesting article jogged some recollections of my own boyhood in the early 1920s and onwards. I then lived with my parents in Higher Tranmere which was then on the outskirts of Birkenhead but, alas, long since urbanised - opposite to our house was a farm, worked entirely by farm labourers and horse drawn machinery. Each spring we would hear the call of the corncrake and, more frequently, that of the cuckoo"*. The location of this farm is only a stone's throw from the Tranmere Rovers' football ground. What a place to hear a corncrake!

Bird artist Charles Tunnicliffe, who grew up on an east Cheshire farm, recalled them in *My Country Book* (1942). His account of a day's haymaking ends with: *"From the uncut grass in the meadow comes the crek! crek! of a corncrake, the sun, sinking redly beyond the distant trees foretells another fine day"*, but, on another page, he confides: *"Corncrakes used to come to the fields every year, but of late I have not seen or heard one of these secretive birds"*. Mechanised mowing had squeezed them out of the fields

From the uncut grass comes the "crek! crek!" of a corncrake.

15

and, now that hay is cut for silage, there is little hope that they will return. Calling males are still occasionally heard, but these have only stopped by on the way to friendlier fields in the far north and west of Britain. In Cheshire, as in most of the lowlands, we can sleep on in the mornings.

Just a few weeks before its report of the first corncrake of 1917, the Chester Chronicle contained this snippet of news: *"...Mr. James Cowley, lock keeper at Hunt's Lock, Northwich, observed an unusual sort of amphibious creature swimming about in the lock, and succeeded in dispatching it. It turned out to be a well-grown specimen of the otter tribe; three feet long from head to tail. Whether it had come up the river or downstream it is impossible to say, but anglers generally will breathe a sigh of relief that the 'poacher' should have met with the fate he deserves".* (7/4/1917).

How attitudes have changed! Recent editions of the Chronicle have devoted whole pages to excited speculation about the possible return of this 'poacher' to our rivers. In 1917, otters were still widespread on the waterways of Cheshire. Although there were no longer any otter-hunting packs within the county, the Border Counties Otter-hounds found plenty of sport along the Dee, Gowy, Weaver, Bollin and Dane. Otters were so common on the Dee that fishermen sometimes found them in their draught nets when they hauled in the catch. Oddly enough, otters had some friends amongst these fishermen who argued that, without this predator to reduce their numbers, eels would soon gobble up all the trout spawn. Most, however, would have concurred with J.D. Sainter's view in *Scientific Rambles Around Macclesfield (1878): The havoc made by these animals in the ponds and rivers is great; for they will go on killing, and eat but a small portion of each fish if it be large, when they find plenty of prey.* The bird-like whistle of otters was heard on the Cheshire meres also, as they hunted the reedbeds at dusk. On the banks lay the leavings of their meals – picked skeletons of bream and scattered mussel shells; their musky-smelling droppings and paw-prints were everywhere.

It was in the 1950s that otter numbers crashed; most people recall their last ever sightings from that decade. On the Dee at Churton, for example, an angler was fishing for eels one moonlit summer night when an otter surfaced in front of him. The two fishermen weighed one another up for a few moments before, with a snort of disdain (quite justified in my view), the otter dived and swam off. None of its kind have been seen there since. In recent years, however, the old signs have been appearing along our waterways once again, giving rise to all those newspaper reports of an otter comeback. The Cheshire Wildlife Trust appointed a full-time *Otters and Rivers Project Officer* in 1994, but she had to wait six years to see her first Cheshire otters - a mother and cub. Otters breed again, but it's too early to get the champagne out. We may not hunt otters with hounds any more, but we thoughtlessly poison their food with pesticides. And what do we do to our rivers? Every year, the banks are stripped of the brambly cover that this shy animal needs, the beds are dredged and motorboats career up and down them for amusement. We must change our own ways before the otter will return for good.

It is far less likely that we will see red squirrels in Cheshire again. Coward and Oldham, in 1910, reported that they were still common in woods all over the county, but retreating from the north-eastern edge of the plain (precisely the area where greys had been introduced a few decades earlier). For years, we have accused these interlopers of ethnic cleansing, ousting the prettier reds from their native woods, but the latest research suggests that a virus wipes out the reds from time to time and, by the time they recover, the greys have advanced a little further. This explains the gradual, east-to-west decline of the reds in Cheshire. A Macclesfield correspondent saw his last one near Disley church as early as 1932, at which time they were still common in Wirral; in 1941, great increases were reported from the Bidston and Noctorum districts. Until about 1950, reds lived in the grounds of Arrowe Hall, Woodchurch (an old-people's home); they were tame enough to venture into the building where patients fed them from their beds. Keepers on Bidston Hill found them tame as well. as one of them told Norman Ellison: *"Yes, we have red squirrels; they are so tame we have to nail wire-netting over the window of our lunch hut. If we left the top open, they would come in and steal our grub".*

But that was their last rally in these parts. An Aldford man, who has worked out of doors all his life, remembers his last red hopping across the road near Aldford bridge in 1951. They clung on for a few years in the conifer plantations of Delamere, where, officially, the last Cheshire sighting was made in 1968. Unofficially, however, a Chester man told me recently, with great conviction, that he saw a red squirrel in his garden in 2002!

Here's another old name that few now remember – foumart. A search through the old Cheshire word-collections turns up some other variants of the name, such as filmot, foomot and fitchet, all of them disguised forms of foul marten - the malodorous polecat. How the village of Marthall must have stunk - it takes its name from the beast!
There was a time when every farm was visited nightly by the polecat, ambushing all the rats and mice it could find. Alas, it was equally adept at slinking into the poultry yard and killing every hen, goose or turkey. For these sins it was trapped by gamekeepers and hunted at night by packs of dogs, so that, as early as the 1840s, people were already talking about *"the last foumart seen in these parts"*. In some districts they lingered on till late in the century, turning up in traps set for other vermin. One live specimen was kept in a keeper's museum at Bramall (about 1870) and those who went about their business by moonlight were still spotting them as late as 1896: *"...polecats are sometimes to be seen in the neighbourhood [Alderley Edge and Wilms*low]. *So an old poacher told me and he knows".* (Cheshire Notes & Queries, March 1896.) One old farmer in Gatley, nostalgic for the polecat hunts of his youth, kept a small bell as a treasured memento; it had hung around the neck of the leading dog in the pack. When Coward was gathering information about them he had to be content with the faded recollections of old men or the stories that their fathers had told about the animal. Many doubted whether it still survived even in North Wales. We now know that it did.

The foumart's woodland cousin, the sweet mart, or pine marten, also found a refuge across the border, where it is now scarce enough to be known as the Welsh Unicorn.

17

They died hard in Cheshire, where they were occasionally spotted during fox hunts or trapped by gamekeepers until late in the 19th century. The last known sighting was in July 1891 when one of these lovely animals was seen in a pheasant field on the Eaton Estate. It was, of course, shot and stuffed and now occupies a dusty corner of the Grosvenor Museum, Chester. The polecat, on the other hand, not only survived but multiplied in its Welsh hideaway. Today, having sniffed the air and found no scent of gamekeepers, it is eagerly resettling the west midland counties - entirely without the help of conservationists. This time we really can start celebrating because polecats are back in Cheshire to stay - a Mouldsworth man tells me they come into his garden! My own scepticism was blown away on Bickerton Hill one baking summer day in 1999 when I came face to face with a beautiful foumart. It glared at me with arched back for a few moments then slipped into a gap in the sandstone wall. *Welcome back!* I said.

* * * * * * * * * * * * * *

In the summer of 2002, I made a pilgrimage to Bagmere, in search of one of Cheshire's rarest butterflies, the small pearl-bordered fritillary, and also curious to see the place where Reverend Pickford heard his bittern on that glorious July day in the 1840s. Like Whitley Reed, Bagmere was drained long ago and is now a treacherous mizzick of sallow, meadowsweet, willowherb and sedge. I stood still for a few minutes, listening to the whispering vegetation, fancying I might hear some faint, old echo of the boom. Before I left, however, two things happened that reminded me that our age is not entirely one of wildlife poverty. Firstly, I met a woman from nearby Brereton Heath who told me that, a few years earlier, her dog had flushed a corncrake from the field in which we were standing. Secondly, she mentioned that two pairs of buzzards nest nearby, birds that are now returning to the lowlands after more than two centuries of persecution. As I pedalled homewards, one of them soared into the blue summer sky, the warm russet of its wings gilded by the sun. An uplifting sight, and one that Pickford, I'll wager, never saw in Cheshire.

The blackbird's rich contralto song sounds beautifully sonorous on a nizzly day.

Chapter 3

Whistling Up the Rain

"Howd yur noise: it allus reens when muck-robins whistlen."

Cheshire is one of the damper counties of this dampish country. No surprise, therefore, that, just as Icelandic has some twenty-odd words for snow, Cheshire dialect has a term for every subtle gradation of rain. If weatherman Michael Fish had a vocabulary like this, his forecasts would be a little more precise and a lot more colourful:

Mizzle (or *dree rain*): Fine rain, barely distinguishable from mist.
Weeting: Light rain.
Mulsh: A more sustained drizzle.
Cowd slobber: Icy rain that numbs the face.
Drabbly weather: Soaking wet.
Slattery weather: Wet and splashy.
Gleamy weather: Hot and showery.
A good sope o' reen: A prolonged wet spell.
A dumberdash: A downpour.
Nizzly: Foggy and damp, etc., etc.

19

Farmers have always wanted to know which of these pleasures was coming next and in the days before meteorology, they had the same blind faith in the significance of bird and insect movements as we have in Mr. Fish and his colleagues. However, science did not win the argument easily. There is a poem in *Warburton's Hunting Songs (c.1860)* in which two Cheshire farmers of different generations and philosophies debate the merits of the new technology:

Farmer Newstyle and Farmer Oldstyle.

"Good day," said Farmer Oldstyle, taking Newstyle by the arm;
"I be cum to look aboit me, wilt 'ee show me o'er thy farm?"
Young Newstyle took his wideawake, and lighted a cigar,
And said, "Won't I astonish you, old-fashioned as you are!
"No doubt you have an aneroid? ere starting, you shall see
How truly mine prognosticates what weather there will be."
"I aint got no such gimcrack, but I knows there'll be a slush
When I sees th'oud ram tak' shelter wi' his tail agen a bush."

Newstyle goes on to demonstrate his new methods of fertilising the ground and his *steam factotum,* a machine seemingly ahead of our own day, for it not only reaps and threshes the corn but ploughs as well. It all ends in tears, of course: the Factotum explodes, spraying death across the farmyard and Oldstyle hurries home, secure in the knowledge that the old ways are best:

"They shanna catch me here again to risk my limbs and life;
I've nought at whoam to blow me up, except it be my woif."

The odd thing is that the aneroid has not entirely supplanted the ram's tail, even today. Almost everyone, it seems, has a pet proverb about the weather. Here are a few wildlife-related saws that I have jotted down from correspondents and acquaintances in the last few years:

Signs of Rain - *Ullets (owls) hoot more than normal; blackbirds "whistle up the rain"; great tits sing their "saw-whet" note; green woodpeckers laugh; the deer at Lyme Park come down from the high moor; brizzes (midges) bite more enthusiastically.*

Signs of stormy weather - *gulls are seen inland in great flocks*; rooks perform a tumbling flight display*; woodpeckers drum; bees and wasps creep into crevices to hide.*

Fair weather signs - *peewits do their display flight*; skylarks sing in flight for a longer time than usual*; bats fly more swiftly; gnats swarm in the afternoon; frogs have brighter, lighter-coloured skins; swallows fly higher*; robins sing from a higher songpost ("Robin singing high - fine and dry; Robin singing low, too wet to mow").*

Now, I take the view that these notions are of interest in themselves. Even if they can all be proved to be nonsense, they tell us something about Man's efforts to understand the natural world through careful observation. Besides, debunking myths is a useful exercise in itself. With that in mind, I wrote to a well-known naturalist/journalist/ broadcaster who, I knew, had been collecting nature-lore in the Cheshire towns for 70-odd years, to see if he could contribute some more. I got a surprisingly nowty reply. Yes, he said, he had files bulging with this sort of nonsense, but he had no intention of sharing it with *"scissors and paste writers"* like me. He had always considered it his duty to sweep away such *"dark-age ignorance"* and replace it with proven scientific veracity. This was a Newstyle, Aneroid man, to the very marrow of his bones.

He had a point, of course, for the more we think about some of these wise sayings, the less wise they sound. Take those storm-tossed gulls, for instance. If they are true gulls of the sea, we ought to sit up and take notice when they are blown miles inland. As I write this (March 4th, 2002), I can see herring- and lesser black-backed gulls, perched on the TV aerials here in Handbridge. The very sound of their chortling calls seems to bring a whiff of sea air and the weather forecast does indeed predict severe gales within the next two days. On the other hand, some of the black-headed gulls that we see throughout the winter months may never have seen the sea! Visit Blakemere, in Delamere Forest, any spring and you will see scores of them, squabbling noisily over nest sites. The meres of Delamere have been their home, on and off, at least since William Webb wrote of *"Puits or Sea Mawes in the flashes"* in 1617. When bats fly swiftly it tells us that there are plenty of moths for them to eat, as there would be during a dry spell, but says nothing about the weather to come. The same applies to swallows. Strong upper winds (which often bring rain) might force their insect prey to fly low, while high pressure would allow them to rise higher, but that, again, only tells us what the weather is doing at the moment. Besides, many people confuse swallows with house martins which fly higher than they, regardless of the weather.

The saw about Lyme Park's deer seems to be a continuation of an old tradition about Lyme's herd of white park cattle (more about them in the next chapter). They, too, were supposed to go up and down the hills like a barometer but, if they did, they were only reacting to present conditions. The tumbling flight of rooks (likewise the calls of owls and great tits) surely has a social function, though they might be more likely to fly this way when the wind is strengthening, as it does when a depression is coming. The idea that blackbirds *"whistle up the rain"* was recorded by Boyd in the 1930s, but a Tarporley woman said the same thing to me, 70 years later. The blackbird's rich, contralto song does sound beautifully sonorous on a *nizzly* day, when *mulsh* is likely to set in later, but is it not simply a case of damp air improving the acoustics? The drumming of woodpeckers certainly echoes through the woods under such conditions. A light-coloured frog may simply be a female, which is generally a little paler than the male. Frogs can expand and contract the pigment cells in their skins to mimic different intensities of light reflected from their surroundings (i.e. they are trainee chameleons), but they do this for camouflage, not to warn us to carry an umbrella.

21

There are traditional methods of long-range weather-forecasting as well, but these fail to deliver so often that it makes you wonder how they have endured to the present day. Here's a selection:

If Budworth Mere has enough ice to bear a duck at the time of Budworth Wakes (mid-November) there will be little frost after Christmas; if it will hold a man by Christmas it will not hold a man after. Only pensioners now remember the winters when dances could be held on the frozen Cheshire Meres. Recent winters have barely provided enough ice to support a robin's weight, so this maxim is becoming obsolete. Incidentally, when Budworth Mere does freeze over, the ducks don't slather about on it for long. Hunger drives them from mere to mere, their numbers swelling all the time, as they search for open water where they can feed. In the harshest weather, they all end up at one place: Rostherne Mere. Why Rostherne? Because, of all the lakes in Cheshire and Shropshire, this is the deepest and therefore the last to glaze over. Here they assemble in their hundreds, or even thousands - mallard, teal, pochard, tufted duck - all thrown together into a thrutching, rackussing quackophony of birds. But if we could translate their chatter into English, they would surely be chatting about the weather they have just been through, not predicting the future.

Big flocks of wood pigeons in winter warn us of a cold snap to come. A retired labourer from Tattenhall told me that his own observations over many years bear this out. Perhaps they do, but what he is seeing is home-grown birds mingling with their Scottish cousins who have fled hard weather in their own land. If snow does follow, it will be brought by a north wind, not by the birds themselves. Redwings and fieldfares are also thought to carry the cold air under their wings. Boyd wrote: *"...their going and coming in spring and autumn are watched with the same interest as a weather-glass".* Remember the farmer in Chapter One who hurried to get his winter wheat in before they appeared in October? He would also be watching for their exodus the following April, muttering: *"We'll not have any warmer weather till the bluebacks have gone".* Again, it may well turn out so, but only because, like other migrant birds, they wait for a fine spell before setting off. In a real Siberian spring, they may even bump into the first cuckoos: *"The people round here call them 'bluebacks', and it was remarked as a curious thing in the late cold spring of 1891 that on April 24th bluebacks were heard on one side of a field and a cuckoo on the other".* (G. Egerton-Warburton - In a Cheshire Garden, 1912).

If frogs croak in February, we're going have a cold spell, sure as eggs is eggs. A Northwich man told me this, with all the authority of long family tradition. But, surely, I said, a cold snap always lies ahead in February! He shrugged and smiled. Most of us, on the Cheshire Plain, live within croaking distance of a marl pit or a garden pond and have heard the bronchitic serenades of the males in early spring. These are sung underwater by gulping air up and down the throat (not open-mouthed on a lilypad, as in the Rupert books), with the puffed-out throat pouch giving it amplification. Females hear the call, plop into the pond and are immediately locked in a passionate embrace which may last as long as 24 hours - but the steamy details of froggy lovemaking need not detain us here. The point to note is that the date depends firstly on latitude (Devonshire frogs may spawn in January while, in Cheshire, February is unusually early for them) and, secondly, on what the weather was like *two months before spawning*. If it was mild and damp, they will emerge from hibernation early and therefore reach the spawning ponds earlier. So when frogs croak in February it probably means that we have simply had a mild, soggy December.

When rooks build high, we can expect a good summer. The Hargrave farmer's wife who told me this had just made me a lovely cup of tea, so it seemed churlish to tell her that a pair of rooks normally uses the same nest for years with a few minor repairs each spring. If they build anew, it tells us only that winter gales have wrecked the old one.

If a robin crosses your threshold, be ready for a harsh winter. A particularly silly one. A robin loses its fear of man only when cold has already driven it to the brink of starvation, not before.

When peewits make their nests on a raised bank rather than the pasture, a wet spell is coming. This reminds me of an old fable. The peewit, it seems, used to build its nest in trees while the wood pigeon nested on the ground. The wily pigeon suggested that they switch places and the peewit agreed. Ever since that day, the wood pigeon has purred smugly, knowing that she is safe from nest-robbers, while the poor peewit laments the bargain with a rueful squeal. And well she might, for, like the skylark, she is now paying a heavy price for life in the open fields. The days when almost every field in Cheshire supported its pair of peewits are gone; today, crops are too often sown in the back-end, so that by the spring they are too high to nest in. Nesting on a bank may be the peewit's best chance, whether it rains or not.

Even the mole, that most agoraphobic of our mammals, is credited by some with meteorological skills. According to Sydney Moorhouse (*Cheshire Life, Nov. 1940)*, a mole-catcher once assured him that when moles abandon lower ground and begin to tunnel uphill, rain is on the way. This is not quite so daft as it sounds. We know that moles can detect water a good distance away, have a strong sense of orientation and can dig at a startling speed, so they are quite capable of making a quick getaway when they suspect a *good sope o'reen* is on the way. However, their first response is to construct a new fortress (a larger hill, containing the nest) in a drier place. The job of digging new runs (which are really food traps) comes afterwards. If a sudden dumberdash does catch them out, they swim for it, using a particularly cute form of doggy-paddle. The same mole-catcher also maintained that if a mole hill is moved during a hard frost or snow, we can expect a thaw before long. New mole hills certainly do appear in freezing weather because, as the worms squirm down into the deeper, warmer soil, the moles have to dig more food traps in order to find enough food, but why should that lead to a thaw?

About 1980, the meteorologist Paul J. Marriott subjected hundreds of these old saws to exhaustive scientific testing and published his findings. The results, at least for forecasting the weather by watching birds and animals, were disappointing, with the long-term prognoses scoring lowest of all. Day-to-day forecasts did a little better, but only a few scored above 50% (those marked in this chapter with an asterisk). That, on the face of it, seems to settle the matter in favour of the aneroid. A few years ago, however, I was talking to a retired gamekeeper (a dyed-in-the-wool Ram's Tail man) about weather lore. He insisted that you have to be outdoors every day to notice the subtle, fleeting clues that nature gives: the direction of a butterfly's flight, snails crossing your path, a fly alighting on your nose. His own pet weather tip was the saw-whet song of the great tit, so I put it to him that this had scored less than 16% in tests, but he merely put on a wise expression and told me that the true countryman sees more than is dreamt of in Michael Fish's philosophy. He may be right. Take, for example, the old Dee wildfowlers who used to go out in punts at daybreak to shoot the ducks, geese and waders of the estuary. If most of the duck flew downriver, they expected a fine day, presumably because conditions were balmy out in the Irish Sea, from which direction most of our weather comes. Similarly, when gulls kept to the windward side of the estuary the fowlers got ready for rough weather. I, for one, would not wish to argue with a hunter who depended for his living on understanding the ways of his quarry. Norman Ellison took the same view: *"A long acquaintance with fishermen, gamekeepers, molecatchers and those who live and work close to nature, has convinced me that they usually know what they are talking about, no matter how vague the reference may appear at first glance."* Cheshire Life, 1946.

Today, I think, most of us put our faith in the aneroid, but we have not stopped looking to nature for clues. Not just yet.

White park bull, wolf and brown bear with skulls of beaver, wild boar and lynx.

Chapter 4

The Last Wolf in England

To Stockport Moor, or Cheadle Heath,
The cavalcades do rattle,
To chase the prowling wolves to death,
Which oft-times steal their cattle.

from *Stockport in Ye Olden Time* (1858).

I am sitting on a hilltop in that slice of the Peak District that mid-Cheshire people still call *the Derbyshire Hills*. In fact, little or nothing of Derbyshire can be seen even from Beeston Castle on a clear day; all those windswept uplands belong to our own, supposedly flat, county. It is truly dramatic country and, while J.H.Ingram was getting carried away when he likened it to *"a bit of Switzerland or Canada"*, only the most blinkered Cestrophobe would call it *flat*. Up here, the drystone walls are built with plenty of gaps to allow the wind to whistle through and, on a day like this, I feel as if I was built the same way. The locals call it a *lazy wind* - it would rather go through you than around you! The very tussocks of grass seem to be clinging to the hillside, lest they be scattered into the sky and tossed about like the tattered crows. Trees huddle in the

25

shelter of valley bottoms. The few whitethorn trees that have found a toehold up here look like blown-out umbrellas but, I suppose, come next May, their crampled, arthritic branches will blossom as well as those in the lowland hedges.

Cold it may be, but at least the sky is clear, giving me a perfect vantage point for surveying the Cheshire Plain that stretches below. This is what H.E.Bates called the *plain-pudding landscape of England*, a homely quilt of farm and field, hedge and tree, the utilitarian foundation upon which the entire English countryside has been built. We think little of it, yet, as Bates pointed out, it is one of the wonders of the world. It has been longer in the building than any of our cathedrals and there is nothing in Switzerland, Canada or anywhere else to match it. However, I have not dragged myself up here to admire the landscape of today: I want to piece together the wilder landscapes of the distant past and track down the wild animals that lived in them. It's time to get into the time machine!

5,000 B.C.

The patchwork has vanished. An unbroken sea of trees seems to have flowed across the Cheshire Plain in every direction, over the central uplands and away to cover the misty Clwydian Hills and beyond. In the valley below us, brown bear cubs are playing boisterously in a tree. Other loud animal voices are echoing through the woods: wild boar snort and snuffle in the cloughs, and stags belder in the clearings. Deer seem to be everywhere - herds of red and small family groups of roe deer. There is another sound that might be taken for the blarting of cattle, but it is the ancestor of that beast, the wild aurochs. The herd's King Bull is an awe-inspiring creature, well over six foot at the shoulder with long, upcurved horns, familiar only from stone age cave-paintings. His coat is a uniform blackish-brown with a white stripe along the spine, while the cows in his harem are a reddish-brown. Other, more familiar mammals are about, too - badgers, foxes, wild cats, martens, stoats, squirrels and, in the rivers and streams, otters and water voles - all of them, even at this early date, very ancient members of our fauna. They all lived here in warmer times, many millennia before, along with the rhinoceros and the hippopotamus.

There are human voices, too, and the echo of stone axes hacking into the trees. Already, there are gaps in the canopy and wisps of blue smoke curling up into the sky. As it grows dark, the woodmen return home and the nocturnal predators venture out. From the rocks above comes a high-pitched skriking: probably a lynx, emerging from its den. A few find a living here, hunting small deer and hares. Wolves begin to howl as the moon rises. It would be wise to move on...

1 A.D.

We have travelled forward five millennia and the view has opened up a little. Now, half the woodland is gone and ploughs are carving up the land. The Weaver, Dee and Mersey rivers wind their way through wooded valleys to the sea, interrupted here and there by the dams, canals and lodges of beavers. Again, we hear the lowing of cattle, but this time they really are domestic herds, though still very different from the placid Holsteins and Friesians that we know today. There is no sign of brown bear or lynx, however. The axe and the plough have driven them away to the far north of Britain; neither will survive on this island for much longer.

* * * * * * * * * * * *

1150 A.D.

Now, trees cover only a quarter of the view. The river valleys are largely cleared of woodland and the beavers, denied their habitat and hunted for their skins, have cleared off with them. Four great hunting forests have been established in Cheshire, one of which is stretched out below us, but even this is like a threadbare carpet, dotted with homesteads and criss-crossed by trackways. Red and roe deer roam freely and, on a distant hill, we can see a fenced park where a herd is kept apart. This is a third kind of deer, recently imported from the continent: fallow deer are the latest fashion in hunting. Wild boar can still be found, but they are staging a last stand against man's persecution.

But listen! From the denser woodland comes that same deep blarting noise that we heard in 5,000 B.C. Has a wild aurochs survived in these woods? No. It emerges from the trees and proves to be a smaller animal, pure white in colour, but with a strong family resemblance. The Romans, some say, bred them from the wild stock and brought them over, perhaps as sacred animals. Whatever their origin, they have since escaped and roam wild in our woodlands.

* * * * * * * * * * * *

1300 A.D.

The population has increased and the woodlands are more and more managed. There is no room now for the white cattle to roam free; all have been emparked and are kept for hunting. The few remaining wild swine have suffered the same indignity. Some fallow deer, on the other hand, have jumped the fence and now outnumber both reds and roes in the wild. Wolves, less dependent on woodland than wild boar, cling on in the hills to stalk the deer. Men, meanwhile, are hard at work on the hillside, digging traps for the wolves. A golden eagle wheels lazily overhead.

* * * * * * * * * * * *

27

The deer parks are still dotted around the landscape, but there is little evidence of wild deer now. Those that do escape are usually killed because they damage crops and make delicious eating. Man is now their only serious enemy, for the wolf has followed the lynx into the history books. Wild cats are still quite common here, but we are unlikely to see one. There are still surprises for the time-traveller, however: an unfamiliar trumpeting call draws our attention upward. Six huge birds - bigger than herons - are flying overhead in V formation with long necks outstretched. They are cranes, departing to Africa for the winter. These are some of the last to breed in Cheshire and within a century they will have abandoned Britain altogether. Now we must return to our own era.

All very well, you say, but where is the evidence that any of these exciting animals ever roamed Cheshire? Well, in the case of bears, beavers and lynx, very little, except that they are all known to have been a part of the British fauna in 5,000 B.C., and Cheshire had plenty of habitat for them. Some animals also had the foresight to leave their bones for us to find. Aurochs skulls have been dredged up from the beds of the Mersey and the Dee and during the excavation of the Manchester Ship Canal, and, no doubt, countless labourers and marl-diggers have been flummoxed by them over the centuries, as in this passage from Beatrice Tunstall's novel The Shiny Night (1931), where some Cheshire yokels have just feyed a marl pit: *"...Mr. Shone proceeded to the inspection of his marl pit. 'Look ye', he said to Elizabeth...'See them stones at bottom - worn round and smooth as turmits, very near? Some on 'em weigh more nor a ton...Times, there's bits of animals mixed up with 'em. You hanna found any, I suppose, Lord Baggily?'*
'Not as yet, Mester Shone. But last pit as we duggen, there was the horns of a great cow.'
'It met have been Noah's flood', said Elizabeth, wonderingly."

Julius Caesar wrote about the aurochs in his account of the Black Forest: *"They are but a little less than elephants in size, and are of the species, colour, and form of a bull. Their strength is very great, and also their speed. They spare neither man nor beast that they see."* I have held in my hands a battered aurochs skull that was dredged out of the Dee at Shotton and, believe me, it's the skull of a very great cow indeed.

The problem with animal bones is that, to be preserved, the animal must either fall into a bog or be eaten by humans. Most of the bones found by archaeologists are kitchen waste. Therefore, the museum has deer bones by the boxfull, but no authenticated relics of wolf, brown bear, beaver, lynx, wild cat or wild boar. Fearsome-looking pig-tusks often turn up on Roman sites, but are likely to have belonged to domestic pigs which, at that time, were almost as toothy as the wild variety. That, however, does not prove that the wild ones were not around as well.

We can follow the tracks of our lost fauna on maps, but be careful: place names delight in dropping banana skins for the unwary. Many of them change over the centuries and must be traced back through old documents before we can be sure of their meaning. Take them at face value and you will soon have an unlikely menagerie - Dromedary Lodge (G.R.76/69), Gibbons Cliff (97/66) the river Croco, etc. Cheshire seems to have plenty of dragons, too, from Worm Hill (93/63) and Drakecar (98/83) in the east, past a couple of Drakelow Farms (69/70 and 73/71) and Dragon's Lane (72/62) to Dragon Hall (48/56) in the west. - enough to keep Bilbo Baggins occupied for years. So, duly cautioned, let's get out the maps. There are a number of wolf names, some of which wear sheep's clothing: Woolley (00/96), for instance, means *wolves'-clearing*. Woolfall (67/45) means either *wolf-hill* or *wolf-trap*, while an ancient field name from Tiverton, Wolfputtes, means *wolf-pits*. There are others, like Wolverham (40/75) and the romantic-sounding Wolf's Edge, but they could as easily be named after Saxons called Wulfhere or Wulfstan. Our most famous wolf name, though, is Wulvarn, a little brook that flows gently through the village of Barthomley. It was near here, according to local tradition, that the last wolf in all England was slain, about the end of the 15th century. If it strikes you as a tame spot for this great predator to meet its end, remember that Cheshire, in the Middle Ages, was a military buffer zone and consequently a haven for outlaws, both human and animal. Wolves do well wherever men shed one another's blood. The question, however, is: does this idea come from an aural tradition, passed down by the locals, or did somebody simply make up a story to suit the name? Without evidence, it must remain a story and nothing more. Barthomley people, incidentally, cherish an old legend about a huge, black dog, as big as a cow which, on dark nights, comes whiffling through the Tulgey Wood with eyes aflame, presaging death. And they expect us to take their wolf story seriously?

Wild boar may be on the map, too. Hog Clough (95/65) and Bar Mere (53/48) both contain the word hog or boar, but whether wild or domestic is difficult to prove. Godscroft (50/76), surprisingly, is a better candidate, since it is corrupted from *galte*, an old name for the wild pig. There is one name, however, which leaps out at us: Wildboarclough (97/68). Here, they say - yes, you guessed it! - England's last wild boar was hunted to its death. It seems greedy and even a little impudent to claim that east Cheshire (rather than, say, Dartmoor or the Lakeland Fells) was the last refuge of both the wolf and the wild boar and yet, if they had to make a last stand somewhere, these lonely hills seem as likely as any of the other places that make the same claim. Once again, though, there is cold water for the etymologist to pour. Some interpret the name as *Clough of the wild bore*, i.e., *wild wind*, and on a day like today it is easy to favour that explanation. Dodgson's *Place Names of Cheshire*, however, favours the more romantic derivation from *wild boar.*

29

Beavers have left little trace on the maps, although Dodgson's *Place Names of Cheshire* records the field name Beaverfield, now lost. Bears were just a memory when most of our settlements were named, so it's no good getting excited about Bearhurst Farm (82/72). On the other hand, we do have a strange fragment of folklore about bears, as Robert Holland of Frodsham noted: *"...there is a curious belief that bears only breed once in seven years; and their doing so causes ill-luck to the breeding of domestic animals. I have it recorded that in 1878 my sow had the misfortune to lose a litter of pigs. Several of my neighbours were equally unfortunate; and the circumstance was gravely attributed to the supposition that 'bears must be breeding this year'."* Was this notion imported from abroad or has it come down to us from our distant ancestors?

Deer names, like deer bones, are scattered thickly across the map. There are the obvious ones, like Deer Stones (02/97), Stag Hall (51/46), Hartford (63/72) and Harthill (50/55) and the ones that we must gawm out, like Wilderspool (61/86), Wildersmoor (68/87), Darley (60/64), Horsley Bank (Congleton, meaning *deer's leap*) and Hattersley (98/94, meaning *stag-clearing*). Some names specify the roe deer: Roe Park (85/58) and Roehurst (63/66). Within the boundaries of the old forests there are names that tell us how the deer were managed. Dorfold (63/51), for example, means *deer enclosure,* while Ashton Hayes (51/69) is the site of *hays* - enclosures within the forest where deer were taken. The odd-sounding Buxtorstoops, in the old Macclesfield forest refers to posts (*stoops*) which held nets *(buck stalls)* for catching roes.

Cheshire is also littered with catty place names, such as Cat's Clough (64/67) and Catton Hall (55/76), but they may simply be named after domestic pussies. Besides, there is evidence that a Cat-Goddess was worshipped in east Cheshire long ago: she may have left her paw-prints at Cat's Tor (99/76) or Catstones (89/63). Wilcott's Heath (a lost place-name, near Wistaston) and field names like Wildcat's Head are more convincing evidence that wild cats actually lived here.

Yarnshaw Hill (98/70), Earnslow Grange (62/70), Yarwoodheath (74/85) and Arley (67/80) all contain the old word *erne,* meaning eagle. Golden eagles last bred in the Peak District in 1688, when there were few people to bother them. Crane names are even commoner, in fact, they are found more often in Cheshire than heron names. But there is a problem here, too. After cranes left for ever, the name came to be used of herons, a confusion that still exists today. The later names, therefore, may refer to herons. Even so, some of the old field names (Cranmere, Cran Moor, Corn Moor, etc.) must, surely, point to the real thing. The most unexpected example, however, is Tranmere, which contains the Old Norse word *trani* (crane). In mediaeval times, it was a watery wilderness where the highest tides flowed right up to where Birkenhead Central Station now stands. And there, long, long ago, stately cranes were mirrored in the water as they bowed and pranced in their mating display. Try picturing that as you wait on the platform! Cranes have not bred in Britain for more than 450 years and, being even shyer of man than bitterns and needing even more fenland to hide in, are unlikely to return.

A third way to trace the fluctuating fortunes of these animals is to examine old documents, particularly those concerned with forest law. For example, a report produced in 1337 for the Earl of Chester found that deer, previously plentiful, had all but vanished from Delamere Forest due to tree-felling for building. Two centuries later, however, Leland wrote: *"Forests, Chases and Parks in Cheshire: I cannot recall any to compare with Delamere, a fine, large forest, with an abundance of red and fallow deer...in the forest I saw but little corn, because of the deer"*. Almost a century after that, James I found both red and fallow deer in the forest when he came to hunt in 1617. We also have the proposal by Charles I to destroy herds of deer which strayed onto farmland around Delamere, although there were said to be some left in Charles II's time. We know of wolves because people were paid to trap and kill them. In 1300, John de Wettenhall was paid 12d (5p) each for three that he had killed in the forest. At the same time, the Cheshire Chamberlain's Account refers to traps set in Macclesfield Forest to reduce their numbers. A charter of 1178-89 mentions wild boar in Bucklow hundred and documents about hunting list wild cats, wild boar, hares, foxes and other woodland animals as beasts of the chase. But here comes another of those name problems: the name *cat* could, at that time, just as easily mean the polecat, the pine marten or even the badger! Even so, it is safe to assume that wild cats were in the woods as well, for they were common all over lowland Britain until the end of the 15th century and lingered in some parts until the 19th, when gamekeepers finished off the stragglers. They have no particular preference either for Scotland or for mountainous terrain, but have simply been driven northward by gamekeepers. There is an obscure 19th century reference to a wild cat trapped in Delamere Forest which may be genuine, since they survived in parts of Wales until 1864. On the other hand, there were lots of feral tabbies around. Harry Neilson, writing in 1935, recalled finding nests of kittens in the undergrowth on the Wirral heaths; they would spit and claw before their eyes were open, just like the purebred wild ones.

The feral white cattle, like deer and wild boar, were kept in parks for hunting right up to the 17th century, for they had retained their ferocity. Their flesh was eaten at special feasts, like venison. Herds were kept at Vale Royal Abbey and Lyme Park and were hunted until about 1700. According to local tradition, both came from wild stock. That is how Egerton Leigh understood it in his poem *The Old Time of Cheshire* (1867):

> *When the wild cattle now confined*
> *Within Lyme's spacious park,*
> *Wandered where'er they had a mind,*
> *Through Maxfield's forest dark.*

An old legend has it that Cromwell's troops drove off the Vale Royal herd when they plundered the Hall, all except for one cow which escaped and returned home and supported the hungry family on its milk. In gratitude, the Cholmondeleys restored the herd and maintained it ever afterwards. The Lyme herd was rounded up every year at midsummer and a few were eaten at Christmas. Local people relied on them as a barometer for, it was said, when they moved up to higher ground fine weather was in prospect but when they returned to the valleys rain was on the way. Both herds gradually declined through inbreeding. Vale Royal's cattle became extinct some time after 1850. The Lyme herd still numbered about 15 at that time but, by 1878, only a bull and three cows remained and they were all dead within a few years. That left only one herd in Cheshire: that at Somerford Park, near Congleton, which had been brought in from Lancashire about 1700. These were disappointingly tame, compared with the other herds and were milked regularly, but the butter made from their milk was highly esteemed. Fletcher Moss wrote: *"They are 'dosome' and a cheese factor of fifty years experience told me the richest cheese in Cheshire came from the Dane Valley"*. Alas, the estate was broken up in 1947 and the herd broken up with it. So ended our last link with the wild aurochs.

And are all the other links broken too? Not quite: a small herd of red deer still wanders in these hills. Roe deer, which died out in 19th century Cheshire, are increasing in Shropshire and Staffordshire and have already bounded across the border: a dead one was found by the road near Chester recently. Surprised? Only 4% of modern Cheshire is wooded, which is pretty bald, even by British standards; how could such a thoroughly-farmed landscape tempt deer? But we are forgetting something: despite the busy roads and new housing, very few people now work on the land. Our countryside is unsupervised and that encourages deer to creep shyly back into places where they once feared to tread. For similar reasons, wild cats are reclaiming parts of southern Scotland. They would be useful allies in our conifer plantations where they might help us to keep rabbits, squirrels and voles under control. They will not find their way here unaided, however, and if reintroduced, they will not stay purebred for long! Beavers and wolves are even less feasible, although there are contentious plans to bring both of them back to Scotland. Wild boar are already present in Cheshire: a free-range herd is kept at Arley, not for hunting, but for its meat. If they ever jump the fence, they will be only too happy to recolonise our woodlands, but do we want them back? In Kent and Sussex, they have burst through electric fences and reclaimed the Weald with a vengeance; free at last, they now pay us back for past persecutions by charging cars and chasing people up trees.

Perhaps we should learn to be patient. History is unwinding at its own unhurried pace and it will, in time, bring brown bears and lynx back to these hills, even if we are not here to see them. One day, I am sure, wild boar will raise their piglets in Wildboarclough and cranes will again be mirrored in the water where Tranmere Rovers were once cheered on. Wolves will howl in the woods where the forgotten village of Barthomley once stood, and they will stalk the deer over the bleak moors of Stockport and the wild heaths of Cheadle. For now, though, I feel safe to open my flask and munch my butties.

Mice have been served in a variety of mouth-watering ways.

Chapter 5

A Frog in the Throat

The chin-cough we call it in Cheshire you know;
Where they cure it with divers recipes in toto.
Some most curious are roast hedgehog! fried mice!
But neither of these you may look on as nice.
Then some hold a live frog quite close to their lips,
'Tis said the frog thus from them hooping cough sips,
An old crone grumbled once, "Her lad's cough would not go,
Though he'd sucked two toads to death," She really said so...

from *Cheshire Recipes for Hooping Cough - Egerton Leigh* (1867)

Egerton Leigh is now best remembered for his *Glossary of Cheshire Words* which was reprinted in 1973, but he also studied local history, archaeology and folklore and, as you can see, wrote some feeble verse. To our modern, vaccinated ears, this catalogue of animal-based cures sounds like a joke, but the chin-cough was no laughing matter. Even as late as 1950 it was killing 400 people a year in England and Wales, mostly infants under the age of two. Today's medical books advise keeping the patient warm in bed and, since the whooping in-breath is often followed by vomiting, to feed him on fluids only. A helping of roast hedgehog or fried mice is not the best way of settling a child's stomach! Killer diseases drive people to desperate measures, however, including remedies that are closer to magic than to medicine. If you think Leigh was making it all up, read this statement from *Cheshire Notes and Queries* (1899): *"There is a superstition in Cheshire that whooping cough may be cured by holding a toad for a few moments with its head within the mouth of the person affected. I heard only the other day of a cure by this somewhat disagreeable process; the toad was said to have caught the disease, which in this instance proved fatal to it in a few hours."* The idea of French-kissing a frog or toad is based on a principle known to anthropologists as *the transference of evil*. The malady (assumed to be a malign spirit) is transferred to another living creature which suffers in the patient's stead. As one old Cheshire woman told the anthropologist Sir James Frazer: *"I assure you, we used to hear the poor frog whooping and coughing, mortal bad, for days after; it would have made your heart ache to hear the poor creature coughing as it did about the garden."* The Golden Bough (1890-1915).

A child suffering from thrush was treated in a similar way. A young frog or toad was washed in running water and wrapped in clean linen before its head was pushed into the baby's mouth for a few moments. As the frog breathed in and out it inhaled the disease. This practice is known from other Welsh border counties and was carried on in Cheshire well into the 20th century; a woman from Tattenhall, interviewed in the 1950s, recalled going through the ordeal as a child. Thrush is a fungal infection which leaves white mottling on the palate and tongue which could be compared to the speckled skin of a frog. If so, the cure may be a form of imitative magic - the idea that an effect resembles its cause and can be returned to sender. The same principle may underlie an unsavoury treatment for *The King's Evil*, known to modern doctors as tuberculosis of the lymph glands. In this condition, the glands in the neck become bloated and inflamed, possibly suggesting the baggy, warty skin of a toad. Whatever the reason, it was bad news for the toad which was chopped in half, one part being buried while the other was carried about by the sufferer.

There are many of these charms which involve keeping bits of dead animals about the person. For rheumatics, try a hare's forefoot or the shoulder-blade of a rabbit wrapped in cloth or paper or sewn into a bag. A neighbour of mine, who grew up in the salmon-fishing community of Handbridge, Chester, told me how, in her youth, the fishermen used to prepare the skins of eels for use in medicine. The older people would lap them up in scarves and wear them around their necks as poultices for sore throats. Another Chester woman remembers people tying them around their wrists for rheumatism.

For consumption, *l'escargot* was on the menu. Readers with nesh bellies may prefer to skip this next passage: *"For many diseases, especially consumption and rickets, 'white snailes', 'shell snayles' and 'earth wormes' were important elements in the medicine, variously prepared and mixed together. The custom of swallowing alive white snails for the cure of consumption is even yet, or was some few years ago, not altogether unknown in some districts of Cheshire."* (Cheshire Notes and Queries, 1900).

Many of these old Cheshire remedies have me stumped for an explanation. What did a jaundice sufferer hope to gain by burying a live frog in a pint mug? Why should warts disappear as a snail, impaled upon a blackthorn bush or buried alive, withers away? Why were young frogs eaten by consumptives? How could dropsy, which is not in itself a condition but a symptom of various diseases, be relieved by taking powdered cockroaches? Did people really swallow woodlice in preference to pills? Apparently they did, and they must have had stronger stomachs than their descendants. I am no arachnophobe, but I would have to be hypnotised before I would swallow *"a fine, fat spider, all alive and kicking"*, as Fletcher Moss put it in his *Folklore* (1898). A spider was a popular cure for a whole range of ailments, particularly the ague, and it was held to work not only for adults and children but also for chickens and pigeons. A generous blob of butter helped it to slip down the throat nicely. Moss added reassuringly: *"If people are at all nervous as to what might happen if the spider came out of the butter when they had swallowed it, I can assure them it was not as bad as the Cheadle Bulldog pill, and it was always said he was a bold man who first swallowed an oyster".* (The *Cheadle Bulldog Pill*, in case you are wondering, was a tiny white pill, no bigger than a pinhead, which, after swallowing, felt as though a live bulldog had been let loose in your stomach. The survivors are said to have erected a fountain in Cheadle in gratitude.)

Of the 640-odd British species, the most valued was the common house spider *Tegenaria domestica,* as championed by the Reverend Dr. Thomas Muffet in the 16th century. Muffet cultivated them in his home and recommended a whole range of medicinal uses, including eye drops of spider urine. His more celebrated daughter acted as guinea pig for his experiments. The history of spider-eating in Cheshire is longer than that, however. They were regarded throughout the Marches as lucky creatures, helpful to man. The herbalist John Gerard, born at Nantwich in 1545, was not so convinced. In his *Herbal* (1597), he recalls: *"...spiders put in a nutshell and divers other foolish toies that I was constrained to take did me no good at all".* Contrast the modern-sounding scepticism of this Elizabethan with the credulity of the peasantry who went on swallowing spiders for another three or four centuries!

Even the cobwebs were not wasted. They were collected on a stick and wrapped around a wound like a bandage to stem the bleeding. This is an ancient practice, recommended by Dioscorides (c.40 - c.90 A.D.) in his *De Materia Medica*, the standard text on medicines for many centuries. Shakespeare's Bottom was another believer:

> *Bottom: I beseech your worship's name.*
> *Cobweb: Cobweb.*
> *Bottom: I shall desire you of more acquaintance, good master Cobweb; if I cut*
>   *my finger, I shall make bold with you.*

A Midsummer Night's Dream, III.I.

Some have tried to defend the cobweb's reputation, suggesting, for example, that it contains an enzyme for hardening the silk which might also coagulate the blood. An arachnologist friend tells me, however, that the spider hardens the silk physically as it spins it. An even further fetched explanation has it that the web contains moulds with penicillin which could act as an antibiotic. What about the bits of decomposing insects hanging on the web? They would soon have the cut buzzing with infection! Happily, there were other, safer alternatives. The blue-veined variety of Cheshire cheese (considered a delicacy today, but thrown out as waste by the old cheese-makers) certainly contains penicillin. It was not eaten, but applied to cuts.

Mice have been served in a variety of mouth-watering ways in Cheshire - they might be roasted, boiled into a broth or baked in a pie. This was once a trusted cure for children who, in Moss's words, "misbehave themselves when asleep" - a Victorian euphemism which has amusingly misled some modern writers. He was talking about bed-wetting. Believe it or not, there was, to a superstitious mind, a logical connection between mice and wetting the bed - a psychological problem that mystified our ancestors. In the days when most houses were infested with mice, they would sometimes be seen scuttering about and over members of the family as they slept. The solution was to make the unhappy child eat mousemeat before going to bed and the smell on his breath was supposed to warn other mice to keep away.

The memory lived on as a mother's threat ("Howd your hush or I'll make you eat mouse-pie!" - enough to make any child wet himself in terror!), but the remedy itself seems to belong to the loveless childhoods of the Victorian era. I certainly never expected to meet anybody who actually remembered it. And then, one day, I met a Helsby woman who did! When she was a girl, in the 1940s, a woman came into her father's confectionery shop, saying that she had heard of this cure for bed-wetting. If she provided the mice, could he put them into a pie for her?

Country people used to make a distinction between traditional cures and charms on the one hand and doctors' physic (or doctor's rubbitch) on the other, and their confidence was not won over easily. Many took the view of the proverbial grave-digger who, when asked by a doctor what he was doing, replied: "Finishing your work!" And if the remedies from 19th century Cheshire seem hard to swallow, take a look at this one from the 17th - a recipe against fevers, jotted down in a commonplace book by John Crewe: "Forty or fifty swallows, when nearly ready to leave the nest, taken and mashed, feathers and all, and distilled in vinegar. Taken by the spoonful with sugar."

According to King's Vale Royal (1656), the secret of good health was in the air: "The Physick of Cheshire: The ayr is very wholesome; insomuch, that the people of the countrey are seldom infected with Diseases or Sicknesse, neither do they use the help of Physicians, nothing so much, as in other countries: For when any of them are sick, they make him a posset, and tye a kerchief on his head; and if that will not amend him, then God be merciful to him. The people there live till they be very old; some are Grand-fathers, their Fathers still living; and some are Grand-fathers before they be married."

One man who got plenty of Cheshire air was Joseph Jones, the *doyen* of Hoylake fishermen, who was befriended by Norman Ellison in the 1950s. He married at 16 and accumulated 13 children, 26 grandchildren and, when he died, aged 94, two great grandchildren. At the age of 93, his only complaint was that he was *"a little hard of hearing"*; other than that, he felt no aches or pains, had no need of glasses and could knit nets as quickly as the young men.

A complete list of Cheshire's creature-remedies would be huge, though still not so big as the catalogue of herbal remedies which do not concern this book. Like antiques and folk-songs, they have become quaint and collectable during the last century or so. But, to our ancestors, they were as everyday as antiseptic and sticking-plasters. Can we be sure that they have all died out? I used to think so, but doubt crept into my mind on August 11th, 1999. On that day, the day of a lunar eclipse, I was walking alongside a hedgerow near Chester when something caught my eye. A big, black pond snail had been impaled on a blackthorn bush at about head height. The thorn had pierced both body and shell. *"As the snail withers, so shall the warts vanish."* I wonder. Michael Drayton wrote of Cheshire folk: *"They of all England most to ancient customs cleave"*. Perhaps some cleave to them still.

A medieval forest was a place for growing deer rather than trees.

Chapter 6

Brown Forest of Mara!

Brown Forest of Mara! whose bounds were of yore
From Kellsborrow's Castle outstretched to the shore,
Our fields and our hamlets afforested then,
That thy beasts might have covert - unhoused were our men.

from *Warburton's Hunting Songs* (1837).

That's how one 19th century hunting man dreamed of the broad, unfettered world of his mediaeval predecessors, and well he might, because the Cheshire Plain changed a good deal during the lifetime of R.E.Egerton Warburton. When the first edition of his popular *Hunting Songs* came out in 1837, the hunting gentry were free to gallop all day, pursuing foxes far over the borders, into Shropshire and Staffordshire; forty years later, when my battered, but much treasured, copy was printed (sixth edition), railways had carved the country into pieces and brought the first unwelcome day-trippers to disturb the dozing villages. Each edition (there were eight during his lifetime) added new songs which, if read in chronological order, show a gradual change in tone from hearty celebration to gloomy speculation about the future of the sport:

Still distant the day, yet in ages to come,
When the gorse is uprooted, the fox-hound is dumb.

In the 1840s, another Cheshire hunting man grumbled: *"....every succeeding year seems to add some new impediment to Fox-hunting. High farming is rapidly converting our fields into gardens...and last but not least in the list of grievances is the scarcity of wild foxes".* That could only be a 19th century utterance, for two reasons: firstly, the modern huntsman, eager to pass hunting off as an essential method of pest-control, would have more sense than to complain about a lack of foxes; secondly, he would not dare to refer to the countryside as *our fields.* What would the huntsmen of the 1840s think of today's impediments, I wonder?

As I write, the day for uprooting the gorse appears to be upon us, so it seems appropriate to write the obituary of hunting here. I hope it will not offend either side in the debate, for I have no wish to feel the huntsman's whip or to be chased across a ploughed field and torn to pieces by a pack of animal-lovers in full cry - I merely want to tell the long, long story of hunting as fairly as I can.

The story begins in those far-off days when the forest of Mara really did stretch from Kellsborrow castle to the banks of the Mersey. Mara made up the northern half (with Mondrem) of the great forest of Delamere, an area almost as big as the Isle of Wight. It was a hunting forest before the Conquest, as was the forest of Macclesfield (formerly known as Lyme), which extended into parts of Lancashire and Staffordshire. When the Normans decided to afforest Wirral as well, perhaps to punish its bolshie people, two fifths of the county were under forest law. Now, before you picture mighty oaks spreading all the way from Hoylake to Chester, let me remind you that the word *forest* has changed its meaning since then. A mediaeval forest was a place for growing deer rather than trees. To create a forest, you drew a boundary on a map, released some deer (if they were not there already) and appointed an army of officials to uphold the forest law. The locals were not turfed out, as Warburton believed; they went on tilling the land and grazing their animals as before. Moreover, the land inside the boundary looked much like that outside it: a patchwork of farmland, heath and moor with coverts for animal safety and pasture for feeding. To get a picture of it, forget the pitiful copse of conifers that we now call *Delamere Forest* and go instead to Little Budworth Common where a fragment of Mondrem survives; this mosaic of heather, bracken, moss, birchwoods and reedy pools is true mediaeval hunting country. Even in Norman times, there were reports of a shortage of wood from all four forests, particularly Wirral where, if the traditional rhyme is to be believed, *from Blacon point to Hilibree, the squirrels leapt from tree to tree.* Well, the American grey squirrels invaded Wirral and made it to Hilbre Island in 1985, but even their compatriots, the flying squirrels could not have done it without touching the ground and our native reds must have had the same problem 900 years ago.

The four protected beasts of the forests were red, roe and fallow deer and wild boar (although fallow deer, being easy to confine, became the favoured quarry and gradually made the other three redundant). These animals belonged to the King and the Earl of Chester who, whether they enjoyed hunting or not, needed an exclusive supply of venison with which to impress their friends at feasts. The master-forester had perks of his own: *"all sparhawkes, marlens, and hobbys within the said forest...all swarmes of bees.. all hounds and greyhounds, to take foxes, heires, cattes, weesel, and other vermyn in the forest"*. That seems to leave precious little for the peasant, who could only watch helplessly as the deer helped themselves to his crops. However, don't believe everything you hear about men being skinned alive for poaching a deer - forest law was primarily a means of raising money, so fines were the usual punishment and the poorest transgressors were often pardoned.

A mediaeval deer hunt was as carefully choreographed as a modern grouse shoot; heads, no doubt, would roll if the King or the Earl of Chester had a disappointing day. What was it like to take part in such a hunt? The best description I know is in the long 14th century poem *Sir Gawain and the Green Knight,* whose anonymous author, to judge by his dialect, may well have been a Cheshire man. Gawain, the purest knight in Camelot, goes off on an arduous quest that takes him through North Wales and the *"wyldrenesse of Wyrale"* (where, incidentally, he meets few that are loved by God or good-hearted men - Merseyside got a bad press even then). After many fights with dragons, wolves, wild men, bulls, bears, boars and giants, he at last arrives at a castle, where he is received as an honoured guest. On each of the next three days, while his wife attempts to seduce our hero, the Lord of the castle goes out hunting, first for deer, then for boar and finally for fox. The description of the deer hunt captures both the addictive thrill and the brutality of hunting, leaving us in no doubt that the poet had experienced it for

The forests of Medieval Cheshire.

himself. As a frosty dawn breaks, the hounds are led into the forest to sniff out the quarry and begin the chase. The deer neezle together in the valley bottoms, half mad with terror, but soon they are driven up to the higher ground where beaters are ready to drive them back towards the stations where the huntsmen are waiting. As they race through, the bows twang and soon the deer are dropping like pheasants at a shoot. Those that slip past are pulled down by dogs and despatched or chased by the mounted huntsmen until nightfall. Such an expensive orgy of slaughter must, surely, have been reserved for special feasts (in this case, Christmas), or the forests would soon have been emptied.

At the time when the Gawain poet was writing, hunting forests were already declining as successive monarchs took less and less interest in their upkeep. Wirral was disafforested as early as 1376, while Macclesfield forest was nibbled away by encroaching agriculture and became defunct in 1684. Delamere lost its deer to a deliberate extermination campaign during the Civil War, although it was not officially disafforested until 1812, after a report described it as *"heath affording a scanty subsistence to a few sheep and rabbits rather than a forest"* (according to the modern definition, that is). After that, it was planted up with oaks and, later in the century, with profitable conifers.

Deer hunting was never confined to the royal forests, however. Cheshire, like all other English counties, was dotted with small deer parks in the Middle Ages. In enclosed, wooded compounds, like the Old Pale in Delamere, the aristocracy farmed deer, providing a year-round supply of fresh venison. They were also milked: when Gerald of Wales passed through Chester in 1188, he saw cheeses, made from the milk of tame deer by the Countess of Chester herself. In Tudor times, deer parks were often the scene of lavish, ceremonial hunts, laid on to impress and entertain important visitors. In the early 17th century, the historian Arthur Wilson took part in a stag hunt at Lyme Hall and gave us this account of his valiant performance: *"Sir Peter Lee, of Lime, invited my Lord* [the Earl of Essex] *one summer to hunt the stagg, and having a great stagg in chase, and many gentlemen the pursuit, the stagg took soyle. And divers, whereof I was one, alighted and stood with swords drawn to have a cut at him on his coming out of the water. The staggs there being wonderfull fierce and dangerous, made us youths more eager to be at him. But he escaped us all. And it was my misfortune to be hindered of my coming neare him, the way being sliperie by a falle; which gave occasion to some who did not know me, to speake as if I had falne for feare. Which, being told mee, I left the stagg and followed the gentleman who first spake it. But I found him of that cold temper that it seems his words made an escape from him; as by his denial and repentance it appeared. But this made mee more violent in the pursuit of the stagg, to recover my reputation. And I happened to bee the only horseman in when the dogs sett him up at bay, and approaching him on horseback, he broke through the dogs and run at mee, and tore my horse's side with his hornes, close by my thigh. Then I quitted my horse and grew more cunning (for the dogs had sett him up againe), stealing behind him with my sword, and cut his hamstrings; and then, got upon his back, and cut his throat; which as I was doing, the company came in, and blamed my rashness for running such a hazard".*

The descendants of those fierce and dangerous stags now graze peacefully in Lyme Park. For that, we can thank the generations of park keepers who, perhaps, have passed down some of the skills of the foresters of Norman times. Inside the hall, you may see an old painting showing the practice of *driving the deer*, that is, forcing them to swim across a pool so that they can be counted. Sitting on his horse, supervising the operation, is the inventor of the method, John Watson; he was the park keeper from 1674 to 1753, and a man whose exploits can still produce a gasp of astonishment to this day. Watson took up his post at the age of 26 and, during his 79 year career (yes, 79, that's not a misprint!), learned to drive deer as easily as a cowboy drives cattle. So expert was he that when his master, Squire Legh, decided to make a present to Queen Anne of twelve brace of stags, Watson readily drove them all the way to Windsor forest, a good 150 miles as the stag staggers and a feat *"not to be adequated in the annals of the most ancient history"*. He also loved to hunt. At the age of 103, we are told, he took part in a chase that lasted six hours and was there at the kill, to the amazement of the younger men. Incidentally, that Lyme-to-Windsor drive won a 500 guinea bet for Squire Legh; I wonder what Watson received for his efforts - a pat on the back?

There are still thriving herds of red and fallow deer at Tatton, Dunham Massey, Eaton Hall and elsewhere, but we once had many more. Some were casualties of the Second World War, when the Ministry of Agriculture had so much land ploughed up for crops. The 300-strong herd at Oulton park, for example, was killed off in 1941 - all except for one, which clung on, commando-like, in nearby woods until it, too, was shot.

Let's leave the subject of deer hunting with a pleasanter story. Harry Neilson's book *Auld Lang Syne* (1935) tells of an eccentric, vestige of deer hunting that went on at Oxton in the 1860s. On hunt days, people would flock in their hundreds to hunt a single hind which was never killed but always returned safely for future use. After a time, she became so blasé that they had to chase her with a stick to get her going. Even more embarrassing were the occasions when, at the height of the excitement, with cries of *tally-ho!* on all sides, someone looked around to find her trotting gently behind them, having run round in a wide circle. At the end of the day, they would take her home in a cart to the comfortable paddock, where schoolboys liked to feed her bread and carrots. Now *that's* what I call a good day's hunting!

To return to Gawain, on the second day of his sojourn the hostess goes hunting for his chastity in earnest, while her husband rides out to hunt the wild boar. This is an altogether more serious opponent than deer. As soon as the boar is flushed from cover, he charges, grunting in fury, and upends three men before galloping away in defiance. When the hounds catch up with him, he turns, slices their bellies open with his tusks, and tosses them aside. The first volley of arrows, bouncing off his thick hide like toothpicks, merely provokes him into skewering a few huntsmen before, again, dashing off. They pursue the boar like this all day until at last, too weary to run, he makes one last charge at the lord, who stabs a sword deep into his throat. Even then, he has to be driven to open ground so that a hundred hounds can pitch in and finish him off. Stirring stuff, but I can see why most retired people prefer a round of golf.

In mediaeval times, boar-hunting went on in Delamere and Macclesfield forests and the enthusiasm long outlived the animals themselves. There is a painting by George Stubbs, showing the first Earl Grosvenor taking part in a boar hunt in 1762, and his descendant Bendor got a taste for the sport in France in the early 20th century. Unfortunately, the rights of the French peasantry were not so easily trampled upon: each hunt was followed by a torrent of angry letters, demanding compensation for ruined crops. That may explain the rumours, around the time of his death in 1953, of a 15-acre *piggery* being built at Eaton Hall. If they were true, nothing came of the plan and the land become a golf course for a time (perhaps the present Duke feels as I do). Today, a herd of 500-800 fallow deer roams the grounds which, in a way, brings us full circle.

On the third day (when Gawain's virginity makes its last, defiant stand), the lord goes off to hunt the fox. Everything in the description is familiar to a modern foxhunter until the moment when the fox breaks cover - then the mediaeval attitudes reassert themselves. Instead of giving the fox a head start in the hope of a good run, they have hounds posted on every escape route, the idea, apparently, being to get the bugger killed as soon as possible. After several hours of twists and turns, the little, exhausted animal blunders into the path of the lord himself, who reacts exactly as he did to the charging boar - by lunging at him with a sword!

There are records of fox-hunting from even earlier than that - in the 13th century, for example, the Abbot of Chester was granted the right to hunt foxes and hares in all the forests of Cheshire - but it was not considered an important quarry. In the words of Sir Thomas Elyot, *"...it is not to be compared with the other hunting in commoditie of exercise"*. With wolves and wildcats as competitors, foxes must have been far less common in that era and, in any case, the hare, with its great stamina and sudden bursts of speed was more popular. As Edward, Duke of York wrote (in the same century as the Gawain poet): *"It is to be known that the hare is king of all venery, for all blowing and the fair terms of hunting cometh of the seeking and the finding of the hare. For certain it is the most marvellous beast that is"*. From the late 15th Century onwards, most country squires and farmers kept a few hounds for hunting hares and the diaries of Cheshire's gentry reveal that some of them pursued their sport almost every day. They also wrote songs about it, centuries before Warburton put pen to paper. A particularly quaint one, in a manuscript of 1615, relates an imaginary 25-mile run across Wirral and North Wales by a talking hare - a route oddly similar to Sir Gawain's. Its title is *"Certaiyne verses wrytten by a Werralyte to ye tune of* [try not to laugh] *upp Willye its tyme to ryse."* The hare begins her journey near Point of Ayr. After a meal of bread and beef, washed down with beer, she sets off, calling, here and there, at the houses of various well-known gentlemen, who set their dogs after her without success. She crosses the estuary in a collier's boat, runs down the Wirral coast, hares through the streets of Chester, over the old bridge, across the marshes and back into Flintshire where, at last, she runs out of steam and is killed. Her dying words are:

I have ben ovr ye world soe wyde
In fflint shire reard in flint I dyed.

43

God send us all in heaven a place
Till everie hare runs such a race;
And ever let us be merrie amonge
And soe Ile Ende my huntinge songe.

For a more realistic view of hare-hunting, we can turn to a song by Charles Legh of Adlington Hall, written in 1751 (and set to music by Handel, who was staying with Legh at the time):

The old hounds push forward, a very sure sign
That the hare, though a stout one, begins to decline;
A chase of two hours or more she has led,
She's down, look about ye, they have her, 'ware dead.
How glorious a death to be honoured with sound
Of the horn with a shout to the chorus of hounds...

Two hours is not exceptional - a good hare might keep its pursuers entertained for twice as long. Hare-hunting in that era was a slow business, often undertaken on foot with stumpy-legged beagles, chosen for their staying power rather than speed. Philip Henry Warburton, in 1740, put it thus: *"We concluded our fox hunting yesterday with a very smart pace & shall now enter upon the sober & less laborious diversion of hare hunting, & it shall be as fatal for any Hound of mine to run fox as mutton"*.

Hare-hunting and -coursing became popular with all classes. Many labourers kept dogs for the purpose and would loose them at any hare they saw. Even a cathedral was no sanctuary, as this excerpt from a Chester newspaper (1784) shows: *"Yesterday morning, January 1, during the time of divine service at the CATHEDRAL, a hare ran thro' the Cloisters and the Broad Ile, and was pursued by a number of people down Northgate Street, and into Eastgate Street, where she was caught by Mr. Spencer, of this city, mason"*

That was no isolated incident, either - here's another, from March 12th, 1823: *"The hounds were in the neighbourhood of the eastern suburbs and a poor hare, supposed to have been frightened from her seat by the 'music', made her public entry into Chester through Foregate-street pursued by a single hound, both very much fatigued. The latter broke down in a very short time, but puss made the best of her way due west. When near the end of Newgate-street a terrier dog caught scent, and set off after puss 'sans ceremonie'. When she got near the Cross a pack was formed, composed of mastiffs, curs, pugs, and all the other canine crew on the spot. The hare continued her course down Watergate-street, and made a bolt near the Linen Hall, where she escaped from the fangs of her pursuers, and, we understand, was purchased from her capturer by MR. HESKETH"*. And there was at least one other case, as recently as 1880: *"Coursing at Chester - on Monday morning a hare was seen in Lower Bridge Street, Chester making its way towards the cross. A labouring man living in the neighbourhood, who has a greyhound, or a dog of that class, slipped the animal at the hare. An exciting chase* ensued. *On reaching the cross the hare turned down Watergate Street, at the bottom of which it swerved to the right along the City Wall, and a kill was finally effected close to the site of the old City Gaol."* If you are thinking that a hare would have to be mad to venture into the crowded streets of Chester, you are probably right - those last two cases both happened in the month of March!

These impromptu chases may, possibly, have been motivated by superstition as well as sporting instinct. Hares, remember, are a traditional disguise of witches; Fletcher Moss knew of people who would scramble across ditches to avoid meeting one, especially in the morning. There is also a widespread belief that a hare running along a town street portends a fire in the vicinity. Chester, of course, is famous for its old timber houses and has seen many disastrous fires in its time.

It was during that same era that packs such as the Royal Rock Beagles (the oldest surviving beagle pack in England) and the Wirral Harriers were formed. Even the famous Tarporley Hunt, the oldest fox-hunting club in England, was founded in 1762 to hunt the hare. By this time, foxes were becoming a problem (newly-planted enclosure hedges = more rabbits = more foxes) but they were efficiently controlled by trapping. Look into the churchwardens' accounts of almost any parish and you should find entries like these: *4s paid for killing 18 foxes* (Whitegate, 1603); *Paid to Thomas Forster for killing of a fox - 1s* (Goostrey, 1648); *Paid for an ould Bitch fox to Will Robinson 2s 6d* (Neston, 1703), and so on. In most places, though, you will be lucky to find one after about 1750. Had the vermin been exterminated? No, the fashion for foxhunting had begun, making *vulpicide* by any other means a crime!

One of the earliest devotees was John Smith-Barry, son of the fourth Earl of Barrymore, who set up his own pack of foxhounds in the 1750s. The Tarporley and Cheshire Hunts were founded not long after, drawing their members from the old county families: Wilbrahams, Crewes and Mainwarings. In some cases, their ancestors had been entitled to hunt in the mediaeval forests and, in the late 18th century, they still felt very powerful. They might not have the power to set aside one third of Cheshire for their sport, as the Normans did, but they certainly felt entitled to prance about the countryside, leaving gates open and breaking down fences whenever they felt like it. Hundreds, even thousands of foxes were imported to Britain from abroad each year - an expensive business which continued, on a small scale, until the First World War. It could be expensive, too, for those who kept ornamental birds, as Mrs. Linnell of Eddisbury Lodge ruefully recalled in about 1874: *"When we came there were no foxes for the hunt, but your father soon altered that. It was rather trying when they ate up my beautiful tame peacock and scattered his feathers all round the farm".* Such valuable animals were not to be killed lightly, which explains this otherwise puzzling entry in the diary of Geoffrey Shakerley, about a meet at Shipbrook in the 1830s: *"they* [the hounds] *found one of the Irish foxes and unluckily killed him".* Copses were planted all over the plain for the pampered foxes to live in. Open a map of lowland Cheshire and you will find it peppered with little green squares with names like Huxley Gorse, Hoofield Covert and Iddinshall Rough. In some copses, such as Handley Sticks, specially constructed *fox castles* were built, made of big logs, covered in branches and made weather-proof with hedge-clippings. The exits even had shutters so that they could be more easily stopped and cleaned out - how does that pest-control argument sound now?

Around Tarporley, it was joked that the farmers reared foxes more lovingly than their own chickens; some, certainly, left scraps out for foxes, just as suburban animal-lovers do today. In 1826, Charles James Appleby wrote in the *New Sporting Magazine*: *"The Cheshire farmers are good preservers of foxes and a blank in their gorse coverts is a rarity"*. What a miserable charade for the tenant farmer - obliged to keep these chicken-eaters alongside his chickens so that the hunt could trample his corn in their pursuit and receive his humble thanks in return! Was he any better off than the wretched mediaeval peasant who could only watch helplessly as deer munched their way through his crops? And what was he to do when a fox took refuge in his cottage? In 1796, one ran into a Lower Peover farmhouse where the farmer's wife (who was frightened of foxes) was drying her husband's shirts by the fire. It grabbed a shirt in its jaws and, in doing so, drew it against the flames and chased about the room, spreading the fire to the curtains and the overhead beams. Before long, the building was engulfed in flame. That, at least, is the story, but I can hear a suspicious echo of ancient mythology in that anecdote. The fox is a traditional fire animal, one of those that are supposed to have brought fire to the earth. According to another tale, a hunted fox once dived into the cellar of the King's Head at Cotebrook, which is why it now bears the name of the Fox and Barrel.

Gamekeepers, in particular, found themselves in an impossible position. One of Egerton Leigh's *Ballads and Legends* tells us what the hunting folk thought of his sort:

It grabbed a shirt in its jaws and chased about the room.

We hold in abhorrence all vulpicide knaves,
With their guns and their traps and their velveteen slaves;
They may feed their fat pheasants, their foxes destroy;
And mar the prime sport they themselves can't enjoy...

The peasantry were expected to look on in wide-eyed wonder. In one of Warburton's songs: *Farmer Dobbin - A Day Wi'the Cheshur Fox Dugs*, an imaginary local yokel somehow finds his way into the exalted company and rushes home to tell his missis all about it:

"'Ould mon, it's welly milkin' toim, where ever 'ast 'ee bin?
Thear's slutch upo' thoi coat, oi see, and blood upo' thoi chin';
'Oiv bin to see the gentlefolk o' Cheshur roid a run;
Owd wench! oiv been a hunting, an oiv seen some rattling fun.'"

...and so he holds forth for 19 verses, full of star-struck admiration for the *Arl ov Grosvenor, Zur Umferry de Trafford an the Squoir ov Arley Haw* before finally confirming his support for hunting: *"Theer's nothin loik Fox-huntin and a rattling Tally-ho!"* How the Tarporley Swan must have rung with patronising laughter when Warburton sang that one! In another song, *Chorus of Liberal-minded Foxes*, the very foxes join in to toast the Master of the Cheshire Fox-hounds, Geoffrey Shakerley:

1st Fox: Here's his health! O'er my old wife he sounded the mort,
    A regular vixen! One of the wrong sort.
2nd Fox: Here's his health! of my firstborn his hounds made their grub;
    His crimes whitened my tag - a most dissolute cub, etc.,etc.

There were protesting voices of course, but few of them have been allowed to go on record. One that did survive is this anti-hunting poster, published some time between 1811 and 1818:

£100 REWARD

*"Whereas the most **intolerable system of despotism** has been attempted to be established over the hundred of Wirral, and a number of foxes have been turned out which have committed great depredations against the GAME and POULTRY, and furnished a pretext for idle and inconsiderate persons wantonly to ride over **Fields of Corn, Clover and Meadow Land** THIS IS TO GIVE NOTICE, that (while the farmers are invited to unite for the protection of their own property by signing a notice to prohibit the hunting for, or pursuing a fox over their lands) the Reward of **One Hundred Pounds will be given on application at the house of JOHN MORRIS, Woodchurch** to any person or persons who will **destroy all the Foxes in the Hundred**, and keep it clear of those noxious vermin, for the **next five years**....*

*N.B. - The few individuals who occasionally join the **Bacon or Herring Hunt in the***

47

Hundred of Wirral, will lose no sport by the extirpation of Foxes, because a Drag, composed of a Red Herring or a Piece of Bacon always has, and will, afford them, after a Mongrel Pack ludicrously kept and hunted, better sport than a wild Fox."

Is a drag hunt really more fun? I find it hard to picture Gawain's host riding out in full mediaeval pomp to hunt a piece of bacon. Incidentally, that *intolerable system of despotism* had been established by Sir William Stanley, who kept a pack of foxhounds at Hooton and seems to have encountered plenty of opposition in Woodchurch. On one occasion, the rector, on hearing that Stanley's hunt was to pay them a visit, had a dead fox hung on the vicarage gate to greet them on arrival (ironically, exactly the same tactic that the hunts now use to intimidate opponents).

But these individuals must have known in their hearts that a propaganda war against the upper crust was unwinnable. A century later, the myth of farmer and huntsmen working hand in hand was still being peddled, as in this quote from *Cheshire and its Cheesemakers* by E.Driver (1909): *"The lordly landowners of Cheshire are very friendly towards their tenants and this mutual friendship secures a zealous regard for each other's interests. The tenant does his part by preserving the foxes for the hunts, and on hunt days, removes the rabbit traps from his fields to prevent the dogs from being trapped. The fox is a serious menace to the farmyard and, apart from fowls, turkeys, geese and even young lambs are carried off."* Read the letters and diaries of huntsmen, however, and another story emerges: Cyril Greenall wrote, during the First World War: *"..I am disgusted with the people round here - more especially at Dutton and Antrobus - they shoot the foxes and then send poultry bills in".*

By Greenall's day, the Golden Age had passed and fox-hunting had entered the modern world with its barbed wire, electric fences, invading suburbs, busy roads and vanloads of anti-hunt protesters. It is easy to see why many now argue that hunting is a relic of a past age and should stay there, along with deer-hunting, boar-hunting and Arthurian knights. But the hunt has changed too. Nobody, nowadays, is awestruck at the sight of titled people on horses, so Zur Umferry de Trafford rides happily alongside Joe Bloggs de Ellesmere Port. In fact, most of the people in pink coats are townies. So, for that matter, are the foxes - they have moved into our gardens and our affections (I can hear the hoarse bark of a fox a couple of streets away as I write this, on a foggy October night). So common are they that hunt supporters, who used to claim that a ban on hunting would soon make foxes extinct, now use the opposite argument: that we will be overrun with them. Many farmers believe that the only way to protect their lambs and chickens is to control them and that hunting is the least cruel method. Yet, it seems inevitable that it will soon be banned on grounds of cruelty. If so, fox coverts will be felled all over the Cheshire Plain, as Warburton predicted, and we will relinquish the last connection with our mediaeval hunting ancestors, who had hunting in their blood. Their rituals linked them to an even more distant time when men hunted to live. Are we about to turn our backs on a part of our own nature? Old Warburton warned us back in 1846 that we would *"regret the past sport that once gladdened the Shire"* and, for once, I agree with him.

They are unnerving creatures, clad in garish metallic lycra.

Chapter 7

"Never Touch an Asker!"

"Notwithstanding the extraordinary efforts already made and still in progress for the education of the masses, and in spite of the incessant endeavours of statesmen and philanthropists to multiply the educational facilities of the people, superstition and ignorance still stalk through the land, spreading moral devastation around."
                                                            Stockport Advertiser, c.1850.

One of my Chester neighbours told me recently that he was having sleepless nights worrying about adders. A friend of his in nearby Aldford had found one lurking in his outside toilet, he said. The banks of the Dee were already snying with them, and the Earl's Eye would soon be infested, endangering our children. This came as a surprise to me for Cheshire has long been known for its relative snakelessness. Some have even suggested that Saint Patrick, who may well have embarked for Ireland from Chester, practised his serpent-banishing skills hereabouts before getting on the boat. Even in the late 19th century, when we had many more mosses and heaths than today, adders were only rarely met with, despite the scare stories that professional viper-catchers used to put about. J.D. Sainter wrote in 1878: *"Forty years ago the common viper was often met with on Danes Moss, but...I believe that this serpent has now become all but extinct in the above locality."* Coward saw them on Carrington Moss in his boyhood: *"Vipers occurred, but we refrained from familiarities, though we treasured the cast sloughs when we found them."* (Bird Haunts and Nature Memories, 1922). In later life, however, he came to doubt their very existence in the county. Talking to gamekeepers and shepherds at the close of that century, he found that few had ever come across an adder. One was caught and killed on Newchurch Common in 1901 and rushed to the Grosvenor Museum in Chester to be preserved for posterity. Even the sharp-eyed Arnold Boyd only saw one before his 50th birthday: *"A snake is a rarity in our county, and many a Cheshire man has seen no more than he would have seen if he had lived in Ireland, and that, as we all know, is none. Till this week I had seen only one, a Viper among the heather, but now I have seen a grass snake too..."* (Country Diary, 12.6.36.) That's one more Cheshire viper than I have seen, although there are reliable reports from a handful of heathy places like Bickerton Hill. Unreliable reports are much commoner, of course, and sometimes turn out to be harmless grass snakes which may be more numerous here than Boyd realised.

So, is an invasion of killer snakes on the way? It seems unlikely, for adders, like other man-eating monsters, have a healthy terror of man. Besides, their feared bite injects only about 0.01cc of venom - the right amount to kill a small frog, mouse or bird, but not a healthy human. Over the entire 20th century, only about a dozen people, usually in very poor health to begin with, died this way in Britain. Any bite is very unpleasant, of course, but most victims are inquisitive dogs, bitten on the nose as they grub about on the heaths of southern England.

According to some of my correspondents, other creatures are to be feared just as much. One warns me of toads: *"...you must not touch them - you can catch warts from them"*, another fears newts: *"...known as the Yellow-bellied Asker, and they are poisonous. Some of them can sting as well"*, while another writes that dragonflies *"sting worse than wasps"*. Others have told me to be careful of lizards (also known as *askers*) and slow worms, which are really legless lizards, complete with detachable tail. For centuries, slow worms have been killed on sight, but those who take the trouble to know them find them harmless and even affectionate. There is a testimony to that in this excerpt from the *Gentleman's Magazine* from as long ago as 1762: *"A kind of reptiles, called by the inhabitants 'long worms' is very common here* [Bromborough] *in the sandy lanes and hedges; and a poor girl who lived here once, fed one of them, which became so tame as to creep around her arm, and receive its food from her without injuring her."* The writer clearly regards the girl as a sort of snake-charmer, toying with a dangerous animal. When our railways were being laid in the 19th century, workmen often found plenty of slow worms as they cleared the ground, but today they are believed to be scarce in Cheshire. However, the records that we do have come from all parts of the county, so perhaps they are simply very skilful at avoiding us. They avoided me until, two years ago, a Chester friend brought one to show me, caught in her garden!

Newts and lizards were placed among the untouchables, too. Boyd wrote: *"A dread of them seems to be universal, and I fear that many are killed by the ignorant. When I was a little boy an old Cheshire gardener taught me to regard them as poisonous...the farm labourer is strangely ignorant in some ways, and regards many creeping things with suspicion; I have been quite seriously warned about handling newts:'Never touch an asker, it'll venom you'".*

Great crested newts do have a nasty surprise for a predator: a nauseating juice exuded through their warty skin that can leave an interfering cat frothing at the mouth. They have other tricks up their sleeves, as well: they can grow new limbs as lizards do, they can even breathe through their skins, but they cannot do us any harm. The crested newt, perhaps because it is so much bigger and uglier than its cousins, has always been the most feared. Some used to believe that it could actually spit venom and even fire (I'd love to see that). Although now alarmingly rare over much of Europe, they are found all over Cheshire - not surprising, as we have a quarter of all the ponds in England and Wales. For that, we can thank the marling gangs of long ago. They dug holes in the fields to extract marl for use as fertiliser, creating thousands of ponds (or *pits*, as we still call them), which are deep enough for newts to breed in.

Askers were also believed to creep into the mouths of those who fell asleep in fields or drank from ponds and live parasitically in the gut. It was not considered far-fetched in 1846, when this report appeared in the Stockport Advertiser:

"On the 7th inst., Joseph Bailey, a youth about sixteen years of age, son of Henry Bailey, of Shadow Moss, in Northern Etchells, vomited a living reptile, of the lizard tribe, the body of which was seven inches long. It was the consequence of drinking at a brook in a field, in which he was at work as a plough driver, in the autumn of 1844, about eighteen months since. He was aware at the time that, whilst hastily drinking he swallowed some object which made him sick, but had no idea that it was anything like what it has ultimately proved to be. From that time his health has gradually retrograded, and he has been subject to fits of vomiting almost constantly, and growing worse and worse. About two months ago he became unable to follow his employment, and was compelled to quit service and return home. He rapidly got worse, upon which his parents called in two surgeons from Wilmslow. While taking the prescribed medicines,

Some believed that an asker could actually spit fire...

51

he appeared daily to get weaker, his sickness increasing, and at this time he was scarcely able to walk across the room. Upon being seized with a fit of vomiting, he threw up three times successively a thick glutinous matter, and at the fourth time of his straining the reptile made its appearance in his mouth, making a desperate attempt to return down the throat, but applying his finger, he laid hold of it and threw it on the floor, and it then ran into the grid hole. In the hurry of the moment his sister so much crushed and mangled it, that further inspection was almost impossible. Since this he has gradually recovered, and there appears no doubt of his ultimate restoration to health." An entertaining story, but there is something suspicious about the sister's eagerness to mangle the evidence!

Like so much folklore, the belief that reptiles and amphibians can live inside us like tape worms was accepted as scientific fact in centuries past. It is mentioned as such in Richard Topsell's *A History of Serpents,* published in 1607: *"But in men's stomachs there are found frogs and Toads. This evil happeneth unto such men as drink water. And Toads are bred in the bodies of men, and yet afterwards these Toads do kill the bodies they are bred in; for the venom is so tempered, that at last it worketh when it is come to ripeness. For the casting out of such a Toad bred in the body, they take a serpent and bowel him; then they cut off the head and the tail; the residue of the body they likewise part into small pieces, which they seethe in water and take off the fat...which the sick person drinketh, until by vomiting he avoid all the Toads in his stomach."*

Both the common and the natterjack toad have been accused of spitting venom at humans, perhaps because of a fancied kinship with snakes (the very name *natterjack* means *little adder*). R. Standen, in *The Natterjack on the Cheshire Coast* (1914) wrote: *"I have heard of more than one case where the unprotected and inoffensive creatures have been ruthlessly slaughtered by ignorant persons under the erroneous impression that they were performing a meritorious act in destroying a lot of vermin."* This, again, was once believed by science. As late as the 1890s, a researcher claimed that, as he examined a frog in his laboratory, it spat in his eye and gave him severe pain for several hours, while toads, he said, could spit enough poison to kill small birds.

Like crested newts, toads can plead self-defence, for they, too, come with a sauce that is just toxic enough to spoil their flavour. Unlike askers, however, they are credited with a saving grace. The following passage comes from Charles Leigh's *The Natural History of Lancashire, Cheshire and the Peak in Derbyshire, with an Account of the British, Phoenician, Armenian, Greek and Roman Antiquities in Those Parts* (1700): *"As this Creature contains one of the greatest Poysons in the Universe, so it supplies us with the richest Cordial. I have in the late pestilential Fever seen repeated Instances, which demonstrate the truth of these: In a low vermiculating Pulse, by giving plentiful Doses of a Powder prepared from Toads, many have been snatched from the brinks of Eternity."* The fact that the toad's main enemy, the grass snake, is immune to its poisonous skin has led some scientists to suggest that it may not be intended for defence at all. It could have a physiological function which benefits the toad, in which case Leigh might have been right about its medicinal value.

Toads have long been seen as contradictory animals, torn between good and evil impulses. Another old notion, widely believed in Cheshire until the early 20th century, shows the supposed inner conflict of the toad in another way. Young toads were supposed to strangle older ones, partly out of sheer devilment, but also as a deliberate measure to reduce their own numbers and so prevent the evil from spreading. I found this difficult to understand until one day, while watching scores of toads mating in the water at Christleton Pit, it all became clear. They were clambering over one another, tangled in the net of their own spawn-strings, the smaller males clasping their portly mates in a vice-like embrace. This grip is not released even slightly throughout the coupling, which may last for several days, and is so tight that his fingers often dig deep into her flesh, leaving ulcerous marks. To my modern mind, they were simply having a good time but, to a peasant mind, steeped in what Beatrice Tunstall called *the half-mystical superstition of the Marches*, it was a struggle between greater and lesser evils.

A few early dragonflies were rattling around as I watched, and I was reminded of the fact that some people in the district still think dragonflies (especially the bigger ones, known as *horse-stingers*) and damselflies keep a sting in the tail. An elderly man from Guilden Sutton told me how they were feared by all the village children when he was a boy. Perhaps this is because, when caught, they twist the body around like a scorpion shaping to sting the captor's hand. They also pair on the wing, in a contorted position which might suggest that they are stinging one another to death. They are unnerving creatures anyway, clad in garish, metallic lycra, their robotic heads swivelling as if on a ball-joint. No flying saucer could outdo the electronic precision of their flight (reaching 40mph) but, then again, they have had 350 million years of practice. Cheshire, again thanks to the marling gangs, is particularly rich in both dragons and damsels: 25 species have been recorded here, 19 of them breeding. But none of them can bite or sting us. On the contrary, they help to rid us of the insects that do - mosquitoes in particular.

Several of my correspondents have mentioned the local name for a dragonfly: *Billy brizz*, with various explanations for its origin. But there is another interesting name which may be older: *edderbowt* (i.e.*adder-bolt*). It may be explained by an odd idea that was widely believed in Cheshire before the war. If an adder was hiding in the grass, an edderbowt would hover directly above it to blow its cover. Why it should want to help humans in this way is uncertain; perhaps, like the toad, it is supposed to have a dual nature. There is evidence that this belief was once widespread and may even have crossed the Atlantic since, in New England, dragonflies are sometimes called *snake-waiters*. If all the dragonflies that hover over the banks of the Dee are pinpointing adders, our children really are in danger!

But our children will not be harmed by dragonflies, frogs, toads, newts, lizards, slow worms or, I am sure, adders. The ignorant scaremongers are the ones to fear. Perhaps, like the toads of popular mythology, they will one day reduce their own numbers by co-strangulation.

In 1903, they were spotted among the spreading beeches of Lyme Park.

Chapter 8

Frem Folk

Before the Industrial Revolution, Cheshire was, by all accounts, something of a backwater. Agriculture was backward and the people, thinly spread across the plain, were said to have *bad luck top end* (i.e., they were a bit thick). They rarely travelled, and when they got wed it was *over the mixen* rather than *over the moor* (i.e., they married locally whenever possible). Their hospitality to visitors was lavish, but newcomers who came to settle were skenned at with suspicion. Such people were known as *frem folk*. Could they be trusted? Those first Manchester cotton barons who set up home in the Cheshire countryside must have felt like the first pioneers to enter Injun Country. But, little by little, the teapot-shaped county began to fill up from the top downwards until, by 1900, it had four times the population of 1800. It was not only humans who found the place congenial: some unfamiliar birds and mammals were putting down roots as well, and the least welcome of them came from America in the year of Custer's last stand...

1876. Before that date, all our squirrels had russet fur and tufted ears. To the foresters of Delamere, they were simply vermin. In the 1850s, for example, red squirrels killed off an entire new plantation by stripping off the inner bark and leaving the trees to rot. Workmen and lads used to kill them with home-made catapults, known locally as *quakers* or *squeakers.* It was a blessing when, from time to time, disease swept through the squirrel population, allowing a few years' respite. They always recovered, however, and the empty woods were always waiting for them when they returned. But, in 1876, something happened which would change all that. It was at Henbury Hall, near Macclesfield, that the rot set in for the red squirrel. Here, for their novelty value, Thomas Brocklehurst released two pairs of eastern grey squirrels from America - the first authenticated record in Britain. They were a little larger than the natives, and brought a touch of American know-how to the job of making good in England. They built dreys in the trees of the estate and began to breed, reproducing more quickly than the reds. They were not so faddy about their food either, scoffing almost any vegetable matter they could find as well as birds and their eggs. Four years later, one was seen at Dunham, nearly ten miles away as the squirrel bounds. The pioneers were on the move.

By the end of that decade, another stranger had been seen and heard, this time on the other side of the county: little owls were breeding on the Eaton Estate. This eight-inch owl is found all over Europe and Asia. In ancient Greece it was sacred to the Goddess of wisdom, Pallas Athene, but the wisdom of introducing it to Britain soon came into question. To the farmer, it was a useful mercenary in the war against mice and voles, but gamekeepers claimed that it also helped itself to game chicks and wild birds.

1880s. Around this time, conspicuous white blobs began to pop up on the hillsides above Longdendale in the north-east of the county. Some 50 mountain hares had been brought south from Perthshire and released a few miles north of the Cheshire border. This was the reverse of the squirrel situation, for mountain hares are the true natives of Britain, ousted from the lowlands by the brown hare which was imported from Europe, perhaps by the Romans. In spring, ramblers were amused to find that, instead of running away at their approach, these hares sat tight amid the green bracken, relying on their winter pelage for...er...camouflage. Were it not for the relentless persecution of buzzards and hill foxes at the time, they would have been picked off the hillsides like snowberries but, with no predators, they soon multiplied and spread southward and eastward. In March 1893, a gamekeeper counted 50 from one spot.

1903. As a new century dawned, the grey squirrels were still hopping from one estate to another. In 1903, they were spotted among the spreading beeches of Lyme Park and, a year later, in woods at Adlington. In 1905, another release, this time at Eaton Park, gave them a toehold in the west of the county.

1908. The Cheshire meres have long been home to another ornamental North American settler - the Canada goose, which was brought over about two centuries earlier. Like the grey squirrel, it has become a pest, for it flies off in great flocks to decimate grass crops and cereal fields. During the 20th century, however, they have been joined by some more welcome immigrants, many of them getting here under their own steam. The tufted duck is one such. These dapper little diving ducks were winter visitors from the

Baltic until, in the late 19th century, some forgot to go home in summer. There were reports of breeding in other parts of the country, so the local birds were watched with great anticipation. At last, in 1908, three little downy chicks were seen dabbling about on Redesmere. Once established, they soon made themselves at home on other meres. Meanwhile, mountain hares (which by now had acquired the imaginative local name *white hares*) had been seen in the hills around Danebower, more than 20 miles south of Longdendale, where they had first entered the county.

Tom Coward and Charles Oldham were writing their comprehensive *Vertebrate Fauna of Cheshire* at around this time - let's see what they had to say. The mountain hare's progress is followed with interest, but there is only a brief acknowledgement of the little owl - one had been shot at Kinnerton, so it had spread only four miles in over 20 years. The grey squirrel doesn't even get a mention! The authors could not have predicted the rapid spread of the grey squirrel and the little owl in another decade, nor the human tragedy that would bring it about: the great cull of gamekeepers of 1914-18. During the twenties, little owls were free to breed all over the Cheshire Plain while grey squirrels leapt into Wirral and earned the title of *pest* for the first time.

1928. In this year, another fluffy chick was attracting attention, this time on Budworth Mere. A young black-necked grebe was heard crying for food as it followed an adult. These exquisite birds had been spreading across north-west Europe for some time, but this was the first sprog to be born in Cheshire. Local bird-watchers had to wait over a decade before hearing such a sound again. Four summers later, our first pochard chick broke out of its shell at Baddiley Mere. Meanwhile, far away in the Balkans, slim, rose-grey doves were preparing something much more ambitious - nothing less than the conquest of Europe.

World War II. Another unfamiliar mammal was hopping about in the eastern hills, this time, an Australian visitor. Some red-necked wallabies had escaped from a private collection in the Peak District and had formed Britain's first breeding colony. They were not expected to survive their first winter. By now, grey squirrels had become a familiar sight in woods where they had not been seen before. One north-Cheshire gamekeeper shot one and took it to a museum, as a cross between a squirrel and a rabbit. Laugh if you like, but remember that the giraffe was once called a camelopard due to the same mistake! The varying amounts of russet in their fur led others to believe that, like the newly-arrived American G.I.s, they interbred with the native species. Not so, but they were certainly over-active, over-competitive and over here.

1950s. It was around this time that another unfamiliar duck began to be noticed on the Dee above Chester - one so improbably colourful that even day-trippers on the pleasure boats could not fail to spot it. The mandarin duck is, perhaps, the ultimate ornamental species; the male looks like a masterpiece of painted origami. Their true home is in China, but they have been kept in British wildfowl collections since the 18th century. In the fifties, a flock was kept on the Eaton estate and allowed to fly free, the gamekeepers releasing about a dozen birds each year to keep up the numbers. A close inspection of the woods revealed that a few pairs were nesting in holes in the trees. By now, the Forestry Commission was offering a shilling (5p) as reward for every grey squirrel's tail. In 1952, 950 were shot in Cheshire; in 1953, 1,934; in 1954, 2,067, but the squirrels soon made up for those losses. Meanwhile, down in Devon, American mink, which had escaped from fur farms, were found to be breeding in the wild...

1959. It took only twenty-five years for the collared dove to colonise western Europe and fly across the channel. In 1959, one was seen at Clatterbridge and, before long, a rickety nest, not unlike that of the wood pigeon, was built at the Wallasey Mariners' Home. A local naturalist reported it and was promptly rapped across the knuckles for giving away its location, but soon they were nesting all over Wirral. The newcomer soon acquired various local names: such as *grey dove* and *French dove*.

1961. The little ringed plover which, until 1938, had not deigned to breed in Britain, reached Cheshire in this year and raised young at Plumley and Sandbach Flashes. By this time, the little owl, or *monkey owl*, as it had become known locally, had gone up in numbers and down in popularity. Norman Ellison wrote: "...*it is one of the few birds I really dislike. To my mind there is something malevolent about its appearance; it looks a 'wrong 'un...'*" (Cheshire Life, 1964). On the other hand, dissection of its pellets revealed that it dines mainly on pests: rats, mice, voles and pestilential insects, along with worms, frogs and miscellaneous mini-beasts. Poultry chicks were rarely found in the pellets, while the wild birds taken were usually undesirables such as sparrows and starlings. Perhaps its looks are against it.

The next wrong 'un to arrive was another controversial American. Ruddy ducks escaped from the Wildfowl Trust's collection at Slimbridge, Somerset in 1960 and were breeding on Quoisley Mere in South Cheshire only eight years later. Like the mandarins (by this time, well established at Eaton), they are difficult to miss, especially in spring, when the drakes rattle their heads up and down like clockwork toys to tice a female into mating. Their aggressive spread was watched with mingled excitement and anxiety. The red-necked wallabies, however, were having a tough time of it. The colony, which had never numbered more than about 50 animals, had been badly hit by the severe winter of 1962-3 and the survivors, all too often, were coming to a sad end on the roads.

It was around this time that a friend of mine swears he saw a little party of hamsters foraging about in the grass at Aldford. Surprisingly, feral hamsters have been seen, on and off, since about 1960, but usually in more urban areas. In their real home, the steppes of eastern Europe and Asia, they live on tree bark, buds, seeds and green plants, so here's another potential pest. Make that two, because some chipmunks were liberated in Cheshire in the mid-60s!

1980s. The first cuckoo of spring seemed to be arriving earlier every year. The reason was that the *coo-coooo-cook* call of the collared dove was now a familiar sound in parks and gardens everywhere. On the meres, pochard and black-necked grebes were also getting better known, while ruddy ducks had produced ducklings on every suitable water

57

in the county. And, in 1985, the warden on Hilbre Island recorded a new mammal species. Yes, the little grey pioneer had hopped across the sands of Dee! This time he really had overstretched himself for the island has no trees to speak of, but there are few pleasanter spots for a day trip.

An Eccleston man told me recently that, one day, back in the 80s, he found a very odd-looking mammal in his shed. Like the gamekeeper, half a century earlier, he described it as a cross (in this case, half-rat half-squirrel) but, afterwards, he looked it up and found it to be an edible dormouse, a species which first escaped from captivity about a century ago. They are well established in the Chilterns, where they have a reputation for raiding lofts and sheds in search of apples. Are they on the move?

1990s. In July 1995, I was strolling along the banks of the Weaver at Hartford, wondering why I never seem to hear the plop of a diving water vole these days, when I came face to face with an answer to my question. The mink stood squarely in the middle of the path and our eyes met. It looked at me as, I imagine, a conquering Norman might have stared down an English peasant: it expecting me to stand aside and let it pass. I stood my ground and, after a few moments, it climbed the bank - slowly, to show it was not scared - and disappeared. That was my first, unsettling encounter with the notorious American invader. An hour or so later, I chatted to a fisherman who said he had to keep the lid on his sandwich box, for the mink were always snooping round. But did they really murder all our water voles or are they, as some say, just scapegoats?

Even our riverbeds are not safe from American interlopers. Take, for example, our native white-clawed crayfish. This is really a freshwater lobster which, though only four inches long, tastes just as good as its marine cousin - it can be made into a soup, eaten like shrimps or boiled in the shell and eaten using nutcrackers. In the mid-1970s, however, crayfish farmers brought in the larger, more economically viable signal crayfish from America. You can guess what happened next. In 1998, the newcomers were found stalking the bed of the Dane, only a mile or two from a colony of white-clawed crayfish, now a protected species. This confrontation can only end one way, for the signal crayfish, as well as out-competing the native species also spreads the crayfish plague, a fungal infection which has already wiped them out over much of southern England.

Meanwhile, the wooded valley of the Dane was echoing with unfamiliar noises - loud barking, squawking and beldering - and people had caught glimpses of a dog-sized animal that seemed half-deer, half pig. Add the muntjac deer to the list! These little Chinese deer escaped from Whipsnade and Woburn at least 50 years ago and, for a long time, were scarcely noticed but, every eight years, their numbers doubled. Sadly, however, muntjac deer are classed with the grey squirrel as one of the forester's worst enemies, so the next sound we hear in the woods may be gunfire.

2003. The problem with these foreign introductions is that, at the time, nobody can tell how a new species will fare. The sad story of the red-necked wallaby has now ended in extinction, so the police will no longer receive calls from puzzled motorists, saying,

"You're not going to believe this, but I've just knocked down a kangaroo..." However, the mountain hare, despite, at one time, being hunted by the Macclesfield and District Beagles, seems to be thriving after a series of mild winters. The black-necked grebe is still Britain's rarest grebe (almost a third of the total breed in Cheshire), but the ruddy duck, on the other hand, is giving us headaches. The problem is that, like many of us, it goes to Spain for its holidays and, also like some of us, sows a few wild oats at the same time, making mongrels of Spain's native white-headed ducks. So, to keep that species pure, our government pays people to shoot ruddy ducks. They do have friends, however: on at least one Cheshire nature reserve, bird-recorders turn a blind eye and list them as *unmentionables*!

Some of the invaders, which at first seemed unstoppable, appear to have over-stretched themselves. Collared doves are now being ousted from some areas by wood pigeons and stock doves, and there have been reports of avenging otters killing the smaller mink. The little owl, on the other hand, is now our most familiar type of owl, partly because it flies by day and partly because (due, perhaps, to our mild winters) it's commoner in Cheshire than elsewhere. And what about Public Enemy No.3? - I refer, of course, to the grey squirrel, which is pipped only by the rabbit and the rat in the league table of destructive mammals. Though a million are culled in Britain every year, they are still munching their way through our hardwoods. However, squirrels that raid litter bins have been picking up fag-ends and now show the first signs of cigarette addiction. Could lung cancer succeed where guns, traps and poison have failed?

There is an interesting footnote to the story of the grey squirrel. The first authenticated record is, as I said, from Henbury in 1876. But take a look at these excerpts from a letter written to the Cambrian Quarterly Magazine in 1830: *"...in some retired glades of Montgomeryshire and Denbighshire...a grey squirrel lives and breeds...The specimens I have seen were as large as a polecat, or a three-quarters grown rabbit; the head roundish, the eyes very prominent, the ears shorter than the common red squirrel's and not the slightest appearance of tufts upon them; the body and legs of a fine grey colour...they are extremely shy on the approach of man, darting through the intricacies of the foliage with amazing swiftness, and taking single bounds of many yards length...I have been informed that the grey squirrel monopolises the woods, and the common red kind are seldom seen near them, which seems reasonable enough, for the size and strength of the grey animal renders him more than a match for the other. I have also seen a very fine stuffed specimen of the Welsh grey squirrel in the possession of a gentleman residing in Chester; it was shot near Llandisilio Hall, Denbighshire, in October 1828."* That sounds like our man - apart from the shyness, which has evidently been overcome over the years. The only way to prove it is to find that stuffed squirrel. Have a look in your attic.

...hiding in the sand, with only its eyes, mouth and dorsal fin showing...

Chapter 9

The Curse of the Stingfish

It's a bright, balmy October day on the front at West Kirby and high tide is only three hours away. A day on Hilbre Island beats a day at the zoo any time, so pack your lunch and get your boots on - we're off!

Ahead of us lies Cheshire's only true wilderness, a place where we are all responsible for our own safety. The only sure route is to make straight for the Little Eye and then to turn sharp right towards the Middle Eye and Hilbre itself. We are not the only day-trippers today and, to judge by the prints of bare feet in the soft sand, many have ignored my advice about the boots. Haven't they heard of the *stingfish*? A surprising number of other mammals also cross these sands from time to time, without actually taking up residence on the islands. Foxes (which have increased hugely in Wirral during the last half-century) often make the trip, though many drown in the attempt. In 1955, a fox killed all the keeper's geese on the island. Weasels are often seen there too, especially in late summer and autumn, when voles and small birds are plentiful. Stoats are rarer, but at least one has been spotted bounding across the sand towards Hilbre. Other animals have been seen at high tide, apparently trying to swim across. A hare was once found trying to cross a deep gutter and, in October 1971, a boat put out from Hilbre to rescue a swimming fallow deer. Don't you believe me? It's true! There are no herds in Wirral, so it must have escaped from some collection in North Wales and swum right across the estuary. It ended its days in Chester Zoo.

Look at the weaving wave-patterns on the sand. Notice, also, the little dimples and worm casts, both of which are made by lug worms which lie under our feet, sucking in wet sand at one end and sieving out the food before squirting it out at the other. You will often see anglers busily digging them out for use as bait. The mud is rich in cockles, too, which are harvested at this time of year by tractor-drawn dredges. Here and there, you may come across a trail of bigger holes. These were made at the last high tide by flounders, which feed on the bottom in a similar way to the worms. Look out for large, diamond-shaped impressions in the sand, as well; these show where a flounder buried itself in the wet sand when the tide went out and swam off when the water returned. Once, believe it or not, these and other flatfish supported Wirral's economy. Look through the old literature and you'll find plenty of testaments to the richness of these waters: *"Wirral is set thick with towns on all sides, but happier in respect of the sea than the soil, the latter not being fit for corn, but the former very plenteous in fish"* W. Camden, Britannia (1586). *"The Dee aboundeth in all manner of Fish, especially Salmons and Trowts. The Marsey, yieldeth great store of Salmons, Conger, Playce, and Flownders, which they call Flounks, Smelts, which they call Sparlings, and Shrimps, which they call Beards."* King's Vale Royal (1656).

Open water fish, like the herring, were caught in the estuary, also: *"At times they [herring] appear in vast shoals, even as high as Chester; they arrive in the month of November, and continue till February: and are followed by multitudes of small vessels which enliven the channel. Great quantities are taken and salted: but they are generally shotten and meagre. It is now about ten years since they paid us a visit."* Pennant, A Tour in Wales (1784). The numbers are much smaller now, but shoals of young herring and sprat still swim upriver each autumn, their presence betrayed by flocks of excited terns.

Yes, Wirral once had a fishing industry to be reckoned with. Hoylake, away to our right, was described, before World War I, as *"... a traditional English fishing port, with its fine fleet of smacks; such a centre as Brixham, Lowestoft or Fleetwood"*. The *smacks* were deep-sea trawlers, about 60 feet in length, which fished the Irish Sea between Cardigan Bay and the Isle of Man. In addition, there were the 32-foot *nobbies*: inshore trawlers, which landed *flukes* (a general name for all flatfish) and shrimps. Big rowing boats, known as *punts*, brought home the shellfish, which were sent out by rail to the big towns. According to H.E.Young, most men in Parkgate went to sea in his day: *"...during most months you may stroll into the place, a lonely Crusoe of the fields, and eight out of ten of the men you meet are fishermen - for the fishery is still good, and yields salmon, soles, and all kinds of flatfish"* (A Perambulation of the Hundred of Wirral, 1909). They were even romanticised in verse:

61

"A group of fisherfolk with southern eyes,
And accents borrowed from a bygone day,
The scream of seagulls and the far-off cries
Of wildfowl flying home from Hilbry way..."

John Pride.

By the 1950s, however, the steam trawling industry was out-competing them. As one old skipper lamented: *"Fishing in these parts is finished. When I was a lad it was a sight to see the smacks setting out - aye, 40 or 50 of them, but nowadays there's only one nobby working and they're hard put to make a living at it".* He and his kind were not forgotten, though. Local writer and broadcaster Norman Ellison (alias *Nomad the Naturalist*) spent many hours listening to their yarns and used them in his BBC Children's Hour programmes on the radio. His stirring tales of eight-foot conger eels snapping a fisherman's leg with one lash of the tail or sharks wrapping themselves in the net and slicing off his fingers were often worked up from true stories heard in the pubs of Hoylake or Parkgate.

We have already reached the Little Eye. From this viewpoint, it is obvious that the three islands are really the high points of a long, rocky reef. To the seaward side of the islands lie rock pools, not as rich in life as those on some other coasts, perhaps, but full of bright things if you look hard enough. Each is a clear, sun-dappled aquarium, a haven for sea anemones in rose or white, starfish, shore crabs, rocklings, blennies, butterfish and pipefish. And nobody can see us out here, so we can act like big kids! The pipefish is easily mistaken for a bit of weed, looking like a seahorse that has been stretched out to a length of a foot or more. It has the local name of *horn eel*, but some know it as the *fish, flesh and fowl fish*, since it has a fishy tail, an animal-like body and a bird-like snout. They often turn up in shrimp nets and, at one time, many a Parkgate cottage had one adorning the mantelpiece, for they can be twisted into fanciful shapes and then dried and varnished. You never know what to expect in these pools. I once found a small octopus, and had to physically drag my companions back to see it before they would believe me. Scoop some algae out and you may uncover a little bullhead, whose sharply-spined fins have earned it names like *sea scorpion, father-lasher and stingfish,* though it is no more venomous than an asker. But that's no reason to be complacent for, hiding in the sand, with only its eyes, mouth and dorsal fin showing, is another, smaller fish, also known as the stingfish, which is, reputedly, the most venomous in British waters. It moves up and down the beach with the tide, lying in wait for shrimps, baby crabs and small fish. It has no quarrel with us, of course - it simply cannot tell us apart from predators. Its official name, *weever*, though it sounds innocent enough, comes from the same root as *viper* and its poison, like the viper's, can paralyse a whole arm or leg. Parkgate shrimpers and fishermen, handling fish all day long, were always at risk and soon learned to put a knife through every stingfish they saw. Once stung, they used to say that the pain would not give over until the tide had reached the same height as it was at the time of the sting (i.e. twelve hours later), although, in fact, it depends on the amount of venom injected. And how painful is it? Well, stung fishermen have been known to throw themselves overboard and there is at least one record of a fisherman solving the problem by chopping off his own finger. A favoured remedy in Parkgate was a poultice made out of the innards of the weever itself - an interesting case of sympathetic medicine, but not to be recommended. If you ever have the bad luck to be stung, let the wound bleed freely and plunge the hand or foot into water as hot as you can stand; then get medical help as soon as possible.

At last, we come to Hilbre itself, where we can climb to view the blue hills, marching rank on rank towards distant Anglesey. Out in the estuary is a broad, sandy bank (the West Hoyle Bank), where a great mass of noisy, overweight holidaymakers appears to have gathered to sunbathe. A peek through the binoculars reveals them as a herd of grey seals, 200 or more strong. In a sense, they really are on holiday, for their breeding ground is Ramsey Island, off the Pembrokeshire coast. Why they swim all this way (all of 170 miles) just to lozzack on this particular sandbank is a mystery, but then again, why do humans travel even greater distances to visit Blackpool? Listen to that babble of voices! Many a boat has set out in the fog to rescue drowning sailors, only to find the bobbing heads of seals, barking happily in the water. On the other hand, many Wirral fishermen used to believe that their voices guided boats through the sea mist to safety. Therefore, just as some river fishermen tolerated otters (see Chapter 2), these men would not kill seals. When, in the 1940s, their livelihood ebbed away, some chose to blame the seals but the small-meshed shrimp trawl is more likely to be the main culprit. The seals, at any rate, have prospered and multiplied here. A century ago, they were very rare visitors but, by the 1930s, up to a dozen might be seen basking together. By the 50s, herds of 100 were common and, two decades later, that number had doubled so, evidently, there are fish here for those with the skill to catch them. Common seals, on the other hand, are very uncommon in these waters. One that was caught on this same bank (c.1894) was exhibited alive as a curiosity and, after death, was stuffed and displayed in the window of an oyster shop in Liverpool. In 1952, a small one found its way into the marine lake and, being unable to get over the sea wall, had to be rescued and released on the tideline. Dolphins and porpoises also find good fishing around here; several species of each have been seen.

Things have been changing since we set out on this walk. Long ribbons of reflected sky are gliding over the sands between us and the mainland. The boats that were heeled over an hour ago are now bobbing on the waves and our pipefish and sea scorpion will soon be freed from the rock pools. A high autumn tide is coming, bringing with it a true wildlife spectacle. At this time of year, wading birds are flying in from the north every day, fleeing the Arctic winter. Some like it well enough to spend the whole winter feeding here while, for others, the Dee is no more than a motorway cafe on the way to warmer coasts. An hour ago, they seemed little more than clusters of dots, far away on the tideline, but now we have only to sit tight and the incoming tide, like an army of beaters, will drive the flocks to us. Ringed plovers (local name: *sand larks*) can be seen paddling through the shallows in short, jerky runs; knots (*duns*) are daddling out towards the tide, then scuttering back rather than get their feet wet; turnstones are turning stones. A flock of dunlins (*sea larks*) flashes around the islands, followed by a more tightly-packed flock of knots and a party of sanderlings. All alight on the only land where they feel safe from us humans: the Middle and Little Eyes. Now, some weightier birds are funnelled in; squabbling redshanks (*whistling plover*), godwits and curlews (*colliers*) descend with all the mingled music of their calls. Most conspicuous are the oyster-catchers (local names: *sea pie* and *cockle-catcher*, both of which suit it better, as it shares the livery of the magpie and it prefers cockles and mussels to oysters). At first, each flock keeps to its own, beaks all facing into the wind, as in many a Tunnicliffe painting. But soon, the sea-spray is flying over the rocks and they are forced to neezle together like Japanese tube-travellers. Every place is taken now, but still the new birds drop in from above, thrutching others aside and knocking the small waders into the foam. Herring gulls descend and bully even the curlews and godwits out of the way. Finally, the Mafia boss himself arrives - the greater black-backed gull, feared by all. He has no need to thrutch, for a space is cleared for him even before he touches down. Having landed, he composes himself, glares menacingly at the little knots (which draw back a little further), then tucks his head away for a snooze. Enjoy this show while you may because, already, the waves are slipping back. As soon as the slob is clear of water again, the birds will all fly off to snap up the newly-exposed lugworms and shellfish.

None of those waders and gulls will stay to nest on Hilbre. Ellison once joked that, of the many thousands of oyster-catchers that winter here, only one will be seen in summer - that on the Hoylake District Council's coat of arms! A few birds do manage to raise young on the main island: skylarks, meadow pipits, blackbirds, song thrushes, starlings, house sparrows and linnets nest here, on and off. Mammals, less able than birds to move on when food becomes scarce, fare even worse. The earliest reference to a mammal

...gawping vacantly, as young children do...

living on Hilbre comes from the pen of John Leland, who visited about 1540. He wrote: "*It is about a mile in cumpace and the ground is sandy and hath conies.*" Those conies had probably been introduced to provide food for the monks that lived on Hilbre in mediaeval times. The first warrens were often set up on offshore islands where it was easier to keep the rabbits in and the poachers out. The writer William Daniell noticed rabbits on the island when he visited in 1813: "*...a few rabbits, the only quadrupeds, to which nature supplies a very meagre provision, only part of the island being covered with a scanty sprinkling of grass*". About 1880, an American had the whim to introduce domestic rabbits (the variety called *Belgian hares*) to Hilbre and they went forth and did what rabbits do best. Despite the scanty grass, they became a nuisance, but it was not until 1933 that the keeper trapped the last one. Their old burrows were taken up by shelducks, which have the appropriate local name of *burrow ducks* from their taste for subterranean nesting. There is no sign of rabbits on the island now. Hedgehogs have popped up at various times since the last war, probably after deliberate introductions by humans. They find life on the island hard, surviving for a few years, then dying out, perhaps because there is not enough food to allow them to stuff themselves before hibernation in autumn. Water voles appeared suddenly in the late 1960s and, although they adapted well to a terrestrial life on the island (and helped themselves to the vegetables in the keeper's garden) they vanished just as mysteriously a few years later. Bats, wood mice and house mice have lived here for longer periods but there are surprisingly few records, thankfully, of rats. There is, however, one mammal that can claim to be a true native of this island: the field vole. If we are lucky enough to see one it will, I am told, be a little smaller and redder than those on the mainland. How satisfying it would be to have our own subspecies (*Microtus agrestis hilbrensis*?) like those on some Hebridean islands! Sadly, their smallness and redness is not quite enough to qualify them as a racial minority but it does, at least, prove that they have a long history on Hilbre.

The seals are in the water now, heads turned towards us, gawping vacantly as young children do. We shall sit down on a rock and gawp back as we pour coffee from the flask. At this distance, they hardly seem like Britain's biggest land mammal, but hidden below each curious face is 25-35 stone of muscle and fat. I was wrong to compare them to children as well, for grey seals are long-lived - some of the females (paler than the males) may even have reached the big 3-0. However much they may remind us of ourselves, seals are the wildest of our mammals, living far out of reach in a hidden wilderness. Fear curbs their curiosity about us and frustrates our curiosity about them. Yet, if we caught a couple and kept them in a tank, what would we gain? In fact, as the sea came in to embrace the island, something much more interesting happened: the seals gained the freedom to view us from every angle, while we are stuck on Monkey Island. Our sense of superiority must go on hold until the seas part again to let us return home. That is one of the things Hilbre has to teach us, and that's why, whatever the weather, a day on this island is better than a day at the zoo.

They nested on the head of a gargoyle that seemed to bawl out in protest...

Chapter 10

The Nightingale Train

In the 1680s, they say, a pair of ravens made their nest on the tower of Over church, in what is now Winsford. The locals already knew what this portended and, not long after, they were proved right: King James II was deposed and sent into exile. How did they know? Because they were all well versed in the prophesies of Robert Nixon (an Over man himself), which stated, among other things, that:

> *When a raven shall build in a stone lion's mouth,*
> *On a church top beside the grey forest,*
> *Then shall a King of England be drove from his crown,*
> *And return no more.*

Robert Nixon was Cheshire's Nostradamus - a gifted village idiot whose predictions had a hold over the British people for centuries. Yet, even if that verse had never been written, the people of Over would have known something unpleasant was afoot, for the raven was a bird of prophecy and his news was never good. His ancient connection with Woden, the old God of the English, caused him, in Christian times, to be linked with the Devil and tarred with the same brush as the magpie, crow, jackdaw, rook and nightjar as

66

one of the *six spies of evil doings*. These birds did Satan's work, so to find any of them raising a brood on a church was disturbing.

In those days, ravens were common birds in the forests of Delamere and Macclesfield but, by the dawn of the 19th century, they were rarely seen, so when, in the 1840s, the villagers of Little Leigh woke up to find ravens flying and croaking around their parish church, it must have seemed doubly ominous. The collective noun: *an unkindness of ravens* tells us that these birds were thought to be alien, unnatural, on the side of death, not life. In Sir Thomas Browne's *Pseudodoxia Epidemica (Vulgar Errors)* of 1650, there is the note: *"The raven, by his acute sense of smelling, discerns the savour of the dying"*. So, although there was no danger of the young Queen Victoria being driven out of her kingdom, an outbreak of fever in the district was put down to their malign influence.

In wartime, people are more than usually sensitised to strange visitations, as I discovered while leafing through the yellowing pages of old Chester Chronicles. It happened in November 1917, when the upbeat propaganda about the war had worn thin and given way to despair and unrest. When big, fierce-looking birds, dressed in dark, iridescent chain-mail, flew above the Town Hall and perched awkwardly on the tower, all the upturned faces on the street below bore expressions of dread. This was seen as a very gloomy omen indeed. No despondency was allowed in the newspaper, of course, so all we find is a debate about the birds' identity, which goes on for several weeks: *"...The strange birds which have been perching on the Chester Town Hall tower made their appearance again last (Friday) evening. There was again a crowd of people interested in their movements..." "Wednesday last was was the eighth day since these large birds were seen on the Town Hall. Each day one or both of the birds has returned, after a few hours' absence, to the same resting place. One of the birds I saw...flying in a sort of semicircle about 100 yards up, but only for a few minutes. It tried to alight on one of the turrets on the north end of the Town Hall, but it missed its grip on the masonry, and slipped down to the lower roof, and I did not get a long enough sight of it to identify the bird. On Tuesday, about 4.30 pm, a number of spectators were gazing up at the Town Hall, and I was glad to have an opportunity of locating one of the birds only, perched on a turret on the south end. It was standing very erect, moving its head and neck from one side to the other, timid with excitement. The sunlight on the bird showed up its colour, size and shape very clearly, and I ascertained it was a cormorant, apparently in its second year." "...It is now generally believed that they are cormorants. A better view of them shows that they have not long legs like herons. They have shorter beaks, and appear to have the webbed feet of wading birds. When they took wing yesterday, their pinions stretched to a great width, and they seemed powerful in flight. The view that they are cormorants seems to be supported by the fact that cormorants have recently been observed on the river."*

I bet you guessed what they were from the description, long before the eye-witnesses which, I think, shows how far the study of natural history has come since 1917.

Cormorants, at that time, were rarely seen far from the coast, so these had probably been driven inland by storms, stayed to fish on the Dee and roosted in the highest place they could find. Today, as any angler will ruefully tell you, they roost around our meres in the winter and, occasionally, stay to nest there. If their legal protection is ever lifted, the sound of gunfire will soon fill the air and cormorants will be mown down like soldiers on the Somme.

It was a bullet that ended the life of a much more exciting fish-eating bird that visited Northenden in the summer of 1865. A young man, who went for a stroll along the banks of the Mersey at hay-making time, heard it in the darkness, *"making a noise like a person vomiting"*. He told his father who, obligingly, returned with a gun and shot it. The bird turned out to be a night heron, a beautiful, nocturnal relation of our larger grey heron. This time, there were no dark predictions (exotic birds bring no baggage of superstition with them), but in its homeland in the swamps of southern Europe, the night heron's harsh cry (which Thomas Bewick also compared to vomiting) used to inspire just as much dread as the raven's. Its Latin name, *Nyctocorax*, actually means *night raven*. A 15th century author wrote:."*By night (as the vulgar think) the Night Raven seemeth with its hateful cry to portend the death of men"*.

Some novel-looking birds popped up all over Wirral.

When an unfamiliar species wings in by the thousand, it is called an irruption, and causes great excitement among naturalists. Such birds are usually asylum-seekers, refugees, fleeing famine in their native lands. In May and June, 1863, some novel-looking birds popped up all over Wirral, mainly on the sandhills near the coast. They made a swift, dramatic entrance, their curving wings making a loud thrumming sound as they sliced through the air. Witnesses likened them to pale-plumaged partridges, but their long, pointed tails and chuckling call were different. They were Pallas's Sandgrouse - not, in fact, a kind of grouse, nor a partridge, but something closer to a pigeon. Normally, they never stray from their home range - the steppes and deserts of central Asia from Astrakhan in the west, through Kazakhstan to Mongolia in the east and south into Turkestan and Sinkiang. Something, probably hunger, had caused them to pour across western Europe like the Golden Horde, plundering any habitat that looked vaguely reminiscent of steppe: sand dunes and stubble fields where they could find spilt grain and the seeds of weeds and grasses. In Cheshire, only Wirral was congenial. A few were seen at Hoylake (shot and stuffed, naturally), Upton-by-Chester, Leasowe Castle (shot and stuffed) and near Warrington (shot again). The survivors stayed until late in the year before returning eastward. A generation later, in 1888, there was a repeat performance and, this time, the sandgrouse built up a sizeable colony at Storeton. The land belonged to a Mr. Brocklebank, who kindly allowed his keeper to shoot a few so that they could be presented to friends as gifts. He hoped that the other birds would breed but, perhaps wisely, they did not co-operate. The last irruption of Pallas's sandgrouse happened in 1909; since then, only half a dozen birds have been recorded in the British Isles. If you want to see one, go to the Grosvenor Museum, Chester, where the bird shot at Leasowe in 1863 is on display. Time, perhaps, has dulled the crisp, patterned livery that once allowed it to melt into the sandy, stony landscape of the steppes, but it is still an exquisite bird.

Even a native bird, if it has been away so long as to have been forgotten, can create a sensation when it suddenly returns in big numbers. Take, for instance, the so-called Common Quail. The male's distinctive three-note call, so rarely heard today, was equally rare a century ago and a century before that. Even our earliest natural historians, like Gilbert White and Thomas Bewick, were hardly more familiar with the bird than we are. Even so, it has an onomatopoeic Cheshire dialect name (*But-for-But*) so somebody must have heard it. During the summers of 1870 and 1893, however, plenty of people had the opportunity, for those were both irruption years, when quail nested in healthy numbers all over the Cheshire Plain. Mr. J. Cash of Northenden wrote, on June 11th, 1893: *"In the river meadows this evening a considerable number of quails called simultaneously; so many, indeed, that I would have found it difficult to distinguish the individual notes. No-one passing along the river bank could fail to be struck by the incessant and curious call-notes of the bird tonight."* Nothing quite like that has been heard in Cheshire since, although hardly a year goes by without some eager bird-watcher hearing a *but-for-but* in a hay meadow or a cornfield somewhere in the county.

Visitations by songbirds are a different matter. They seem to be welcome everywhere, even in time of war. Take this observation of W.H.Dobie at the time of the Boer War: *"The Lesser Whitethroat continues to increase in Chester and the neighbourhood where, a few years ago, it was a species by no means common. It frequents gardens in the heart of the city; amid the chorus of horns, bells and voices which woke sleeping Chester on the morning of May 31st, proclaiming the fall of Pretoria, its laughing note was heard within a hundred yards of the Town Hall".* Not so much a harbinger of doom as a lucky talisman!

Nightingales visit Cheshire only rarely but, when they do, we give them the star treatment. In April, 1865, one was heard in Lymm and created such interest that, in an early example of wildlife tourism, a special Nightingale Train was started to bring people from Manchester to hear it. Can you guess the bird's eventual fate? Of course you can. Only a couple of years earlier, there had been similar gatherings of rapt listeners in Birkenhead Park. Harry Neilson, who was an excited child at the time, described the event in 1935. His parents took him along night after night to join the growing throng and hear the liquid notes, warbles and trills coming from some tall trees in a shrubbery. One night, the crowd crept forward, hoping to catch a glimpse of the legendary songster. At last, they saw him, sitting high up on the branch, with a china bird-whistle in his mouth. Fortunately, this young man had a good turn of speed, or he might have ended up in a glass case along with the Lymm bird.

Crowds of listeners can do more damage than they realise. In April 1896, the gardener at Oakwood Hall, Romiley heard the unmistakable rich and varied song of a nightingale in the woods and the news soon spread. The cock bird sang all through May, attracting an audience which grew bigger every evening until, at last, the owner lost patience and had the damned bird silenced by firing blank cartridges. That put an end to the performances, although, happily, the gardener later saw the hen bird taking food to the nest. A Barnton farmer found a more lucrative solution when, in May 1936, a nightingale sang for a week or so in a small clough on his land. Boyd wrote: *"...I listened to its song on the 12th of May, a privilege rarely granted in Cheshire. Its presence was soon noised abroad and brought in a nightly audience of hundreds, so many indeed that the farmer...stopped trying to keep people off his crops and instead made a charge for walking over them. There was no evidence of its nesting, but a small boy confidently showed me a wren's nest on a tree trunk as that of the nightingale".*

In the Middle Ages, nightingales may have been common in the coppice woodlands that fuelled Cheshire's salt industry. Since then, they have slipped southwards until, by the 19th century, Cheshire lay just north of their normal range. Today, they have a *Never-North-of-Watford* mentality or, at any rate, rarely cross that imaginary line that runs from the Severn to the Humber. There has been at least one unsuccessful attempt to reintroduce them: some were released at Jodrell Bank many years ago, but they never returned. The odd thing is that, if you look through local bird records, there seems to have been a surprising increase in nightingales in the 1960s. People were hearing them everywhere, particularly in towns. In 1962, for instance, one was singing only a stone's throw from Chester Town Hall, just like that lesser whitethroat. The mystery is all too easily solved, however, for it was around that time that street-lamps came to be left on all night. Robins and thrushes, thinking dawn had arrived early, were singing their little hearts out all night, as they still sometimes do. The belief that all nocturnal singers are nightingales dies hard and has given many a sedge warbler a moment of fame. Here's an exercise you might like to try: go out on a fine May night with a volume of Keats in your pocket and approach a marl pit or rape field. You are almost sure to hear a sedge warbler, a bird which sings both day and night (*night sparrow* is one of its Cheshire names). Now, as you listen, read a few verses of Keats's *Ode to a Nightingale* and ask yourself if that thin, scratchy song could have inspired such poetry.

Almost every spring, somebody, somewhere in Cheshire, is lucky enough to hear a real nightingale, often in the Bollin or Dane valleys. These are usually bachelor birds that have strayed too far north and failed to find a mate but, no doubt, eggs are occasionally laid.

On a cold day in March 1996, I was approaching Chester Town Hall when I heard - no, not a nightingale - but a resonant, guttural cry that instantly transported me to the wilds of Snowdonia. A pair of ravens had flown over to Chester and done a little house-hunting. Town Hall employees had been puzzled by the sticks that littered the front steps each morning and it was several days before it occurred to one of them to look up. In the niche on one of the turrets that flank the clock (near where the cormorant lost its footing, nearly 80 years earlier) a voluminous nest was being built, strong enough to withstand whatever the wind, rain and sea could throw at it. Two months later, the healthy youngsters stretched their wings and launched out over the upturned faces of onlookers (wearing happier expressions this time!), in search of discarded chips and kebabs. The following spring, they moved house again, this time choosing the cathedral tower which, no doubt, appealed to their gothic tastes. They nested, not in a lion's mouth, but on the head of a gargoyle which seems to bawl out in protest against the droppings that trickle over its face. Since then, they have raised young every year.

Contrary to what you might have read, this is not the first occasion since the 16th century that British ravens have nested on a building, and they were not the first to re-enter Cheshire - the successful pairs at Beeston Castle and Helsby Hill beat them to it. They must, however, be the most celebrated birds in Chester's long history. The city's tourism department was quick to add them to its list of attractions, so much so that some suspected it of fraud. One man, who was (and, for all I know, still is) convinced that they were mere crows, wrote to me, expounding an elaborate conspiracy theory! But Chester's new mascots are already an institution, enshrined in papier-mâché and carried aloft in the annual Midsummer Watch parade, along with the traditional giants and mythical beasts. And there is a happy irony about ravens nesting on a gargoyle, for our ancestors carved such monsters to scare away the devil (and his six spies, including the raven) from God's house. Yet, today, even the canon will tell you that he loves to hear the croaking overhead as he takes Holy Communion. We have progressed from superstitious fear, through curiosity, to affection and even commercial exploitation.

One final point about birds and prophesies: things are not always what they seem. Not all big, black birds are crows, nor all nocturnal singers nightingales and, of course, the sound of vomiting in a pub car-park is not always made by a night heron. We should not believe everything we read, either. It is almost certain that Robert Nixon, for all his fame, never existed, so there is no need for Charles, Earl of Chester, to look up at the cathedral tower with a heavy heart.

The colony on the Dee marshes has a lamentable history of egg stealing.

Chapter 11

Fluking, Snigging and Egg-stealing

"Better belly burst than good meat lost"
old Cheshire proverb.

This chapter, I fear, will displease some of my naturalist friends and all of my fellow vegetarians. It is about the eating of creatures not normally found on the supermarket shelves - a disquieting idea, but one that has a long history. In times of hunger, when people think more laterally about food, many species of bird and animal find themselves on the menu for the first time, and Cheshire, well within living memory, has had its share of hungry poverty.

Why do you smile? Have you accepted the media's sneering image of Cheshire: a well-fed county, entirely populated by brash millionaires, and the green-wellied gentry? If so, it's time you met some of its poorer people, in towns like Crewe, Runcorn and Ellesmere Port. Cheshire is, statistically, one of the most average counties in England and could stand as a microcosm of the nation, for it has a bit of everything: crumbling industrial towns, leafy suburbs, new towns, picturesque villages, scruffy council estates and sleepy farms. Its proportions of rich and poor, blue-collar and white collar, employed and unemployed are close to the national average, too. I think we have been scapegoats of the inverted snob for long enough.

As I was saying, hunger was a problem in these parts until surprisingly recent times. If you doubt it, talk, as I have done, to some of the old-timers who lived through the depression. In those days, wages were often painfully low, especially for rural workers. Shropshire farmers used to joke that their Cheshire neighbours lived *"at the better end of the pig-trough"*, because they subsisted on potatoes and buttermilk rather than beef and beer. No surprise, then, that poaching became an accepted institution. Imprisonment held no fears, since it brought the guarantee of a square meal each day. As Old Long Jone, the *King of the Cheshire Poachers*, used to tell his younger, more headstrong mates in the 1890s: *"Awlus give in when you're fairly ta'en. Better a whol skin wi' six months than a hangin' dooment. And besides, they han us to keep when we're i' prison!"*

When first planning this book, I intended to devote a chapter to the story of poaching in Cheshire, but soon gave up the idea. Finding material about poaching in the old days was no problem: I soon had enough scribbled notes to fill a whole book, never mind a chapter. No, the difficulty lay in getting information out of today's country people. No matter how garrulous they might be on other subjects, one question about poaching and they would shut up like clams! However, one day, at my local gym (of all places), I got chatting to a lifelong poacher who was more than willing to tell me about his activities. To my disappointment, he didn't talk like Old Long Jone and, judging by his waistline, getting a square meal was not a problem for him either. We happened to be talking about the need to control grey squirrels and I learned that he has his own solution to that dilemma. He eats them! He finds them delicious. If that thought makes your flesh creep, remember that, centuries ago, the native version was considered a delicacy. If greys are just as tasty, why not eat them to compensate for the damage they do? But there was more - he told me that fox meat is also very good. Surely, I asked, you don't eat foxes? No, but he has found buyers for the foxes that he kills and they tell him that the taste is akin to that of lamb. Foxes, like grey squirrels and rabbits, are more numerous today than ever before, so we can spare a few for the table. The poacher has also eaten a few hedgehogs in his time, using the following gypsy recipe:

Baked Hedgehog

After gutting your hedgehog, singe off the prickles over the fire and scrape it all over with a knife. Then, stuff it with sage and onion and sew it up. Finally, plaster it with clay and cook it over the fire until the clay cracks; then your hedgehog is ready to eat.

The hedgehog's flesh has been described as *the finest meat in England*, so why not give it a try? During my researches, I turned up an interesting old reference to hedgehog eating in the *Macclesfield Courier (1812);* the writer, G.R. Mannion, claimed that Cheshire's gypsies, who never strayed beyond the county boundary at that time, always left a plateful for the fairies when they had finished.

73

What else could we serve up, I wonder? Arnold Boyd had a neighbour who dined on rat pie quite regularly, but that seems unlikely to catch on with the public. A pity, because rats now outnumber us and their population is rising. How about mice? In 19th century Cheshire, it was not unknown for house mice to be eaten, as we shall see in a later chapter; they taste a little like rabbit, I gather. If your cabbages are ravaged by snails, remember that they too were food for the poor until relatively recent times. Try the common garden snail (Helix aspersa) - the Romans used to enjoy that species, and they should know. Almost every species of bird has been eaten at some time in the past. While passing through Ashton Hayes recently, I met a very respectable farmer's wife whose father used to go out on rook shoots and afterwards eat them in a pie. She gave an involuntary shiver as she said it, but I gather that rook pie is as tasty as pigeon pie. Sparrows, also, have often found their way into pastry, as several old folk have told me, though they hardly seem worth the plucking.

My poacher friend is especially partial to eels, which he nets in the River Gowy and eats sliced up and fried in butter. I have met a few Cheshire people who like them boiled, casseroled or even poached in milk, but the general preference for fried eels (sometimes topped with a fried egg) is suggested by the old Cheshire proverb: *I've other fish to fry than snigs* (eels) *without butter.* They are not to everyone's taste, of course. One of my correspondents, from the Malpas area, writes: "*Eels - you mean Sniggs. My mother can recall Sniggs to be caught at Edge Mill and being eaten by her father, mother and brother. She did not like them - the silver ones are the best, the others tasted muddy*".Happily, another letter, from a Wirral fisherman, supplies the answer to this problem: "*Eels should be kept alive for three days in running water to clear them of muddy taste*".

Favourite eel-fishing spots were once important enough to be mentioned on the maps. Elton, near Ince (and also Elton Hall, near Sandbach), means *farm where eels are got,*

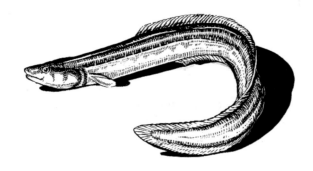

while Snig Hall (Lach Dennis) and Snig Hole (a field name at Walton, near Warrington) preserve the old name. Countless people have told me where and how they landed their eels. Around Farndon, they'll tell you that *snigs as long as your arm* used to be caught in the pits around there. At Huxley, children would gather at the water mill (now defunct) on the Gowy and open the gate to lower the water level, then wade in and do their best to catch the slathering snigs with their bare hands. On Frodsham marsh, children would sometimes dam a ditch just before the water reached a bridge. The eels, which had congregated in the bridge's shadow, were soon left stranded and easily caught. A different approach was to scoop out a hole in the bottom of the stream and wait for the eels to gather in it. Then you could make a trident from three fingers of your right hand and plunge it in - a child's version of the eel-pole with its four serrated teeth.

However, the subtlest way of catching snigs is to *snig* for them. Many of my Handbridge neighbours are, or used to be, fond of snigging and each seems to have his or her own variation on the theme. One man swears by this method: thread about 30 lob worms onto a length of worsted; then roll it all up into a writhing ball of worms and tie it to a line. Next, attach the line to a short stick and lower the worm-ball into the water until you feel it touch bottom. Now comes the patient bit. Raise and lower the stick a few inches, very gently, until you feel a bite; then yank it out onto the bank. Your snig, with its backward-pointing teeth caught in the worsted, should come out with it. This man's grandfather, who grew up in Neston, used to catch eels in marl pits, using a less labour-intensive technique. He would use a weighted line, baited with a boiled Parkgate shrimp, and tie the end to a nearby willow sapling. The springy branch bent just like a fisherman's rod when the bait was taken. The prize for the simplest method of snigging, however, goes to another Handbridge man. As a boy, he and his mates would slat a grassy sod into the river and pitch it out later in the day, by which time it would be wriggling with elvers. A man who grew up on a farm at Bretton recommended yet another way of snigging: *"You want to get a bit of cotton wool, mix it up with flour and water, stick it on your hook and dangle it near the bottom,"* he said, looking very serious. *"Have you caught many that way?"* I asked. *"No, never got one!"* he replied, with a laugh, leaving me a bit perplexed. The Dee salmon fishermen, on the other hand, knew what they were about and caught huge eels in the river. Many all but lived on salmon, flatfish and snigs until, in the 1960s, their livelihood began to flounder.

At Stretton Watermill, near Farndon, you can see a restored eel trap of a type once used on many Cheshire meres to provide eels for the tables of the gentry. These were set at the end of April, when eels begin to ascend our rivers, although the biggest catches are made on dark, drabbly nights in October. It is then that the adults swarm into the rivers to begin their astonishing 3,000-mile Atlantic crossing to the seas where they were born. Pickmere, Quoisley Mere and others became famous for their bounteous harvests of eels. So plentiful were they that, at one time, many were packed into barrels and sent to London to be jellied, while many more were consumed in the Lancashire cotton towns.

Lampreys, still common in most of our rivers and streams, were once very popular as food and were fried in butter, just like eels. They are strange, over-simplified fish, with no ribs, scales or even proper fins. In place of jaws, they have powerful sucker mouths which are used to latch onto other fish or mossy stones. Our three species are known officially as the s*ea lamprey,* the *lampern* and the *brook lamprey*, but I have come across a confusing variety of local names, such as *lampon, ninny-nine-holes, blood-suckers, silver eels* and s*and pride.*

The best-known lamprey gourmet is King Henry I, who died as a result of stuffing himself with them, against the advice of his doctors. I have not yet come across a living lamprey-eater, but there were evidently plenty in the past, as these two snippets from the *Cheshire Sheaf* (1880) prove: *"Sixty years ago lampreys were caught at Ince, and brought to Chester market in panniers by a woman on horseback"*; *"Within a few years I have seen it* [the lamprey] *taken in quantities from the causeway, at Chester, and offered for sale at the Cross".* On the river Weaver, at Northwich, there was a favoured spot for catching them, as mentioned in Ormerod's *History of Cheshire* (1819): *"...a stream or brook (now covered by a plat) called Lamprey Ditch, which formerly abounded with fish of that name, but which the increase of navigation on the river Weaver seems to have totally destroyed."* The *plat* (bridge) was where the Town Bridge now stands.

Some old books contain recipes for lampreys baked or stewed in port wine, but today's anglers regard them strictly as bait. Some of my neighbours remember the days when fishermen collected them as bait for catching eels. Lampreys would congregate along the weir at Chester to feed among the stones, looking like hundreds of silver strings trailing in the fast-flowing water. The men had to approach them very gingerly from below the weir (for the fish would feel any turbulence in the water) and pick them off wearing old gloves or woollen socks so as to get a purchase on their slippery bodies. At Farndon bridge, they used special wooden *lamprey-tongs* to wrench them off the pebbles. Some local people remember paddling about, looking for *stocking needles* (eels) and *blood-suckers* (lampreys) when they were children. *"Haven't seen any since the sixties"*, say the old folk, but perhaps their eyesight is not what it was, for lampreys still find their way into the salmon-tagging station at Chester weir.

The stone loach is another fish that seems too piddling to bother with as food but which, if caught by the sackful, is a rare delicacy. Known in Cheshire as *Tommy Loach,* it can be found nosing among the pebbles in most fast-flowing streams. Here, again, we can find evidence for loach-eating on the map. Loach Brook, which flows into the Dane, near Congleton, must surely be a place where they were taken.

Speaking of place-names, I wonder how many residents of the Chester suburb of Flookersbrook understand the meaning of the name? Centuries ago, when the Dee estuary lapped almost to the walls of Chester, *Flokars Brook* was one of its many tidal tributaries. Flounders (or *flukes*), which spawn out at sea, spend the winter in fresh water, so they would pass through these brooks in spring and autumn, providing a rich harvest for the *flookers.* In 1635, there were several fisheries with *flookenetts* in the area. Flounders are still common in the Dee, and swim upriver as far as Farndon (I know a man who has caught them at Shocklach). As with eels, there are different methods of fluking. Down the estuary, lads used to use the now illegal *dicky net* (perhaps similar to the old *flookenett*) which was staked out before high tide to intercept the flukes (and the occasional bonus - a mullet, sea bass or salmon) as they swam in and out with the tide. In the meantime, they would collect *samkin* (samphire) to be eaten as a boiled vegetable with the fresh fish. A Heswall man told me that his cousin was once fined for using a particularly grisly instrument called the *drag* - an iron bar, fitted with big cod-hooks was scraped across the bottom of a channel, impaling the flatfish as they lay in the sand. Chester fishermen had a similar, and equally illegal, device called the *rake*, which looked like an overturned bed of nails. I know a woman who tried it in her youth and remembers feeling the horrible vibrations through the handle as the poor flukes struggled to escape. The sporting way, of course, is to catch them with your bare hands. At West Kirby, for example, the marine lake is drained from time to time so that its bottom can be cleared of mud. This leaves just one puddle where the flukes and eels are forced to congregate in their hundreds. On one occasion, in 1965, Norman Ellison watched as men and boys collected more than a thousand big flounders.

In the springtime, wild birds' eggs are an obvious source of food. Even today, when so many pits have been filled in, we have about 6,000 breeding pairs of moorhens in Cheshire, each laying 2-4 broods of 8-9 eggs each year. The nests, usually built on a tussock of rushes, are out of the reach of foxes and weasels but not children, who used to tie a spoon onto the end of a broom handle and wade out until they could ladle out one of the speckled eggs. The prized egg was then carefully passed to a pal who waited on the bank. Almost all the older countrymen and women that I have spoken to remember this pastime with nostalgia. They also remember dropping many eggs into the water and leaving their socks behind in the mud. One old farmer confided that most of his expeditions had ended this way! The more successful usually boiled the eggs and ate them back home.

On the great estates, wild birds' eggs used to be gathered systematically by the gamekeepers. At Tatton, for example, moorhen eggs were made into meal for the pampered pheasant chicks until about 1960. But peewits' eggs were the real delicacy. In the 19th century, they were sold at market in huge numbers and, in more recent times, they have been in demand at upper-class banquets. One of the gamekeeper's more tedious duties was to quarter the fields and gather as many as he could find. Since, in the early 20th century, almost every field had at least one pair of peewits, there were plenty left over for the humble labourer as well. The eggs are superbly camouflaged, of course, and would be almost impossible to find, were it not for the frantic distraction display of the parents which, though it may fool foxes, stoats and weasels, merely leads humans to the right spot. So long as the collectors were not greedy, the birds could maintain their numbers: this correspondent had the right idea - *As a child on the Wirral (Meols) in the early fifties we used to take one egg from the then abundant lapwings' nests and fry them over an outside fire. It is difficult now to visualise how common lapwings were in those days".*

77

Not everybody was so fastidious as to take only one, of course, and the population began to fall. Over the last 15 years, however, numbers have halved and it is not egg-pilfering but modern farming that is to blame. All the peewit asks for is a pasture or a spring-sown field where its eggs can be laid and its chicks can forage for insect food, but many modern farms cannot provide even that. Crops are often sown in the back-end so that, by the following spring, they are too tall to nest in. Likewise, the grass grown for silage is so pumped up with fertiliser that, by April, it is already a dense jungle; then, in May, the machines move in to cut it, crushing chicks and eggs as they go. Yet, the farmer has a great friend in the peewit. It probes the soil, feeding on wireworms, leatherjackets and other larvae of destructive pests that lurk just below the surface. T. A. Coward, writing in 1935, went so far as to link Cheshire's improved agricultural prosperity at that time with the 1928 *Protection of Lapwings Act*, the first official recognition of the bird's good work. Have today's farmers forgotten their old ally?

There is another, perhaps more romantic, reason for respecting the peewit: I wonder how many of those egg-gatherers knew that they were, in effect, collecting Easter eggs? Our distant ancestors believed that these eggs, seemingly strewn randomly about the fields were a gift from the Goddess Eostre. In the springtime, she would take the shape of a hare and run over the land, laying eggs as she went. Today, we remember the Easter bunny and the Easter egg but the peewit's role in our pagan traditions has been all but forgotten.

Black-headed gulls' eggs used to be collected and eaten, too. We usually think of them as sea birds but, compared with other gulls, they are land-lubbers, finding much of their food far inland. They prefer the company of peewits and rooks (two of their Cheshire names are *peewit gull* and *sea crow*) and, like them, they have learned to follow tractors, snapping up the tasty grubs that are turned up by the plough. Some of them, as I mentioned in Chapter 3, also nest many miles from the sea, usually on islands in the middle of a mere or on a wet marsh. Here, they are out of the reach of foxes but, sadly, not humans. One old colony, on the Dee marshes, has a lamentable history of egg-stealing. Here, the nest sites are all too easily reached and, like peewits, the gulls give the game away by swooping on intruders. In the 19th century, local people took the eggs as casually as we would pick blackberries and one Burton woman earned herself the nickname *Jinny Catch-a-Gull*. The plunder continued in the 20th century too. In 1936, G. B. Griffin complained bitterly about the thieves who went home with baskets piled high with eggs: *"Laying commences at the end of April, or early in May, incubation lasting about 21 days, but so many clutches are destroyed that the nesting season is prolonged indefinitely until the birds weary of the struggle against hopeless odds."* (Cheshire Life, Jan. 1936).

I know a Little Sutton man who admits to many wrongdoings in his youth, including egg-collecting on Burton Marsh. He and his mates only robbed nests that had just a single egg to be sure that it was newly laid. He found them good eating, with a stronger flavour than a supermarket hen's egg. They also took redshank eggs which, he says, were plentiful all over the marsh at that time (probably true, though reliable records are scanty). Incidentally, a local name for the redshank is *whistling plover*, which reminds us that their eggs, like those of other waders, such as oyster-catchers, used to be sold under the name *plovers' eggs*, being similar in taste and appearance. Duck eggs were not taken but, when the young were *flappers* (i.e., could flusker about but not quite fly), an old rabbit net was stretched across one end of the pond. Dogs then approached gingerly from the other side, driving them into the waiting net.

There was once a time when men could make a good living from wildfowling on the Dee estuary, as we shall see in a later chapter. It was famous for its wild geese, but today only feral Canada geese are seen in any numbers. As a pest species, they ought to be in the gunner's sights but, according to my egg-stealing friend, local wildfowlers are loath to shoot them. He asked a friend why and got an interesting reply: *"I know of only one recipe for Canada geese and I'll give it you":-*

1 Canada goose, plucked and dressed
2 Onions
1 Shoe (black or brown)
Fat

Stuff the goose with the onions and the shoe. Cover it in melted fat and cook it in a low oven (c.160°C) for 3 hours. On removing the goose, take out the onions and shoe and put them on a plate. Finally, throw the goose in the bin and eat the shoe!

While chatting to all these people, it seemed to me that a tone of relaxed contentment came into their voices as they recalled the fluking, snigging and egg-stealing of days gone by. It belonged to a simpler, slower, less neurotic age when there were fewer moral questions to be grappled with. Those days are lost forever but the subject of wild food, oddly enough, has come back into conversation. It is, after all, a very *green* way of getting your dinner: it provides fresh air and exercise, it saves resources and, if we confine our predation to pest species we are helping the farmer and the forester. We could begin with the obvious candidates (rabbit and wood pigeon) and perhaps, when our stomachs are stronger, move on to the less obvious (rat, fox, mink, grey squirrel, etc.). Besides, there is a satisfying naturalness and a pleasure in using your own skill to catch your tea. I saw it clearly in the face of one old farmer as he recalled fishing trips with his mates before the war. On gentle summer evenings, they would set off with their home-made eel-poles and, as dusk was falling, return home with their catch and enjoy a supper of stewed eels and mushrooms.
"That was in the Good Old Days", he said.
*"Don't you mean the **so-called** Good Old Days?"* I asked.
"No", he replied, with a wistful remembrance, *"they **were** good days"*.

These no-nonsense men had seen a sea monster.

Chapter 12

The Hoylake Monster

One would not expect sea-monsters to figure strongly in the folklore of a county like Cheshire which, though not entirely landlocked, has only enough salt water to dip the spout of its teapot into. The smacks of Hoylake used to be out at sea for up to six weeks at a time, but they were never in danger of sailing over the rim of the world or likely to come home with stories of krakens or giant serpents. Yet, over the centuries, gigantic creatures have appeared in our waters or on our beaches that no-one, at the time, could explain.

In 1636, Sir John Bridgeman, Chief Justice of Chester, was riding his Lent-Circuit when he came upon a monster cast upon the sands of Dee. It caused such a sensation that a broadside ballad was composed in honour of this *"strange (and miraculous) Fish, cast upon the lands on the meads, in the hundred of Worwell, in the County Palatine of Chester (or Chesshiere). The certainty whereof is now related concerning the said most monstrous Fish.*

> *Of many marvels in my time I've heretofore,*
> *But here's a stranger now in prime that's lately come on shore,*

Invites my penn to specifie what some (I doubt) will think a lie.
O rare beyond compare
In England neer the like.

It is a fish, a monstrous fish, a fish that many dreads,
But now it is as we would wish cast up o'th sands i'th meads,
In Chesshire; and tis certaine true describ'd by those that did it view.
                                                                    O rare, etc.
Full twenty one yards and one foot this fish extends in length,
With all things correspondent too't for amplitude and strength:
Good people what shall I report doe not account it fained sport. O rare, etc."

The next ten verses give detailed measurements of the monster. It is five yards high and too heavy for twelve yoke of oxen to stir, though some plan to float it to land when the sea turns. A man on horseback has stood in its vast mouth and its jaw-bone is five yards long with 34 teeth, each weighing over 2lb. Sixteen tons of oil have already been taken from its head and there is plenty more where that came from. Its *pissle* is four yards in length and as thick as a man's torso, while its *cods* are as big as hogsheads (casks). Its tongue is *"so mighty large, I will it not expresse, lest I your credit-overcharge"* (personally, I'm too impressed by the 12 foot *pissle*, to care much about the tongue). The song concludes:

"When he upon the sands was cast alive, which was awhile;
He yelled so loud, that many (agast) heard him above sixe mile:
Tis said the Female fish likewise was heard to mourne, with horrid cryes.
                                                                    O rare, etc.
The Mariners of Chester say a Herring-hog tis nam'd:
Whatere it be, for certaine they that are for knowledge fam'd
Affirme, the like in ages past upon our Coast was never cast. O rare, etc."

Now, south Wirral, at that time, was a sparsely-populated country, known to outsiders as *Gobbinshire*, from the supposed dimness of its people. Having seen nothing like this before, they named it the *Herring Hog*, as if it were some colossal, fish-eating pig. But, for all that, their description of the beast is accurate enough to make it clear that it was a sperm whale, and a full-grown bull at that. The only puzzling statistic is the number of teeth. According to my copy of Herman Melville's Moby Dick: *"There are generally forty-two teeth in all; in old whales, much worn down, but undecayed; and not filled after our fashion"*. The Herring Hog was eight teeth short of this total - perhaps his dentist had extracted a few.

Schools of sperm whales roam all the tropical oceans of the world, rarely straying into colder waters. The few individuals that wander as far north as the British Isles are thought to be younger bulls that have been driven out by older rivals. To find a mature male in the shallow waters of the Irish Sea was, indeed, rare beyond compare and would cause a sensation even today.

In 1659, a comparatively small monster was found by the Dee fishermen: *"June 23, 1659, a great fish, the length of 3 yards, was taken upon the Sands in Saltney, after this forme - The fines on it back, taile, and under it belly of the same substance of the fish, the colour on the back is black and shineing like unto iet, and the belly very whit"*. The harbour porpoise, which is particularly common in our waters and often washed up, fits this description best, but it might also have been a dolphin. In those days, it was important to know which, because, due to a silly law, all dolphins, whales and sturgeons were classed as Royal Fish, giving the Earl of Chester first claim on them. In 1357, two Wirral men were fined for selling a dolphin without first informing the Earl (though one was later let off because he had fought at the Battle of Poitiers the year before!) and in 1498, a Hilbre monk found himself in the dock for the same crime.

But it takes a real giant to get the public excited and, in 1782, one duly appeared, as reported in the Chester Courant (14.5.1782): *"...while some fishermen were casting their nets for salmon, about two miles beyond the Lower Ferry, near to this city, to their unspeakable astonishment they observed a FISH of uncommon size rolling about, a part of its body appearing above the surface. The tide, having then been some time ebbing, had left an insufficiency of water for its enormous bulk. On the approach of the boat it appeared extremely agitated, its strength being nearly exhausted by the want of its natural element, and the length of time it must have been beating about in this situation. One of the fishermen very resolutely jumped on its back, and, cutting a hole through the dorsal fin, fastened a rope through it, by which means they, on the return of the tide, floated it up, with the help of two boats, to the new Crane. There, with the utmost difficulty, they effected its landing, not less than ten horses being employed for that purpose. When brought to shore, its form and size struck every person with inexpressible amazement; many opinions were given by seafaring men and others respecting its species - several pronouncing it a basking shark, others a spermaceti whale* [i.e.sperm whale], *and others a grampus* [dolphin or porpoise], *to none of which (as described by our modern writers on Ichthyology) it bears any certain similitude. The length of it is 25 feet; the girth proportionately large, though very unequal; it has two dorsal and six pectoral fins - two of the latter of a very singular form, partaking of the nature of feet. The tail is perpendicular, of prodigious size and strength; there are five gills on each side. The mouth, when opened to its extremity, is three feet wide; there are not any teeth, but a vast quantity of small, irregular, sharp prominences, which are evidently given it for the purpose of comminuting its food, the orifice of the throat being astonishingly narrow for a creature of such magnitude. The upper and under jaws are each furnished with ten strong protruberant bones, horizontally placed, which meet when the mouth closes, in such a manner as to appear capable of breaking almost any substance. The eye is situated very near the mouth, and scarcely larger than that of an ox: the nose is hard and prominent; the whole body is covered with a very thin skin, and the weight of the fish is between four and five tons. We have been thus particular, as it is probable that some ingenious naturalist may favour the public with the certain information of its real species."*

This is another easy one, for the prodigious fish herein described bears a most certain similitude to a basking shark. I only wish I could write to the editor of the Courant and tell him so but, after 220 years, I may have missed my chance of glory. The description is so exact that the author's confusion with whales and dolphins is surprising; evidently, those *modern writers on Ichthyology* were not much help! A full-grown basking shark is truly huge - as long as a bus and as heavy as a white rhinoceros. Beachings are unusual and have led to excited talk of *sea-serpents* throughout history. In drawings, those foot-like pectoral fins are sometimes exaggerated into real feet, complete with claws. In fact, they are the male's *claspers* which are used to introduce sperm into the female during copulation. Unlike the *Herring Hog*, Chester's basking shark had not lost its way; its descendants still enter the Irish Sea every summer and congregate around the Calf of Man. Here they may be seen cruising just below the surface, mouths open, sifting plankton through their gill-rakers. Where they spend the winter months is a secret that the writers on Ichthyology have still not uncovered. Perhaps they hibernate on the ocean floor. Nobody knows.

That was not the last basking shark to sunbathe on the sands of Wirral: in May 1930, a slightly bigger one dumped itself on Egremont promenade and another was stranded at Meols in October 1953. The first of these, when local children had finished bouncing about on its bloated carcass, was cut up small and converted into chicken feed - a disrespectful end for the world's second largest fish.

...cruising just below the surface, mouths open, sifting plankton...

A killer whale, captured by two fishermen at West Kirby in March 1876, suffered a similar fate. Scientists hurried to the scene, only to find that the body had already been sliced up and boiled down for oil. Witnesses could tell them only that the monster, in its death agony, spewed up heaps of sea-fowl feathers. Killers are not unusual in British waters and may be seen at any time of year. They do eat seabirds as well as seals, porpoises and fish.

Sometimes, the disposal of the body can lead to legal difficulties, as two salmon fishermen of Handbridge discovered in 1928. In August that year, Joe Johnson and Tom Totty found a huge hole in their net when they dragged it out of the water. Other fishermen had noticed the movements of some creature for the past week and were debating whether it was a whale, a shark or a porpoise. The following day, with the help of half a dozen other men, they set out to catch it, as the Chester Observer (25.8.1928) proudly related: *"The type of sea monster which had for a few days in mid-August exercised the minds of Dee fishermen and occasioned a good deal of perturbation and speculation was definitely settled on the evening of 14th Aug. when Mr. Joseph Johnson, senior, and Mr. Thomas Totty, junior, both of Greenway Street, fishing with their net in the stretch of water between the Grosvenor road bridge and the railway bridge, Chester, landed a royal sturgeon. The big fish made a gallant fight for liberty and tore the net literally to pieces in the struggle."*

Like salmon, sturgeons swim up rivers to breed, but this one had lost its way; it had probably come from the Baltic. Johnson was tickled to death by his catch: *"We got him in the best way we could and by letting him do as he liked...I was proud to land him...It was the sight of a lifetime to see him in the water."* The fish was then killed and, after some curious rituals (due, no doubt, to the sturgeon's ancient status as a *Royal Fish*), handed over to a local fishmonger. It stayed in his window while they held a *Guess-the-Weight* competition, with the proceeds going to charity. By the time the fun was over, the fish was unfit to eat and all was wasted. A pity, as its flesh is considered a great delicacy and said to taste like fish, flesh or fowl, according to which part of the body it is cut from.The weight, incidentally, was 136kg and the length 2.48m - about average. An elderly neighbour of mine can just remember, as a girl of four, seeing the famous sturgeon and, on another occasion, a porpoise which was killed by the fishermen and lay in state in her grandmother's kitchen!

Sturgeons had been put on show before: in 1899, for example, one was netted by a Parkgate boat and exhibited in a nearby barn, where the public paid 3d a time to go in and marvel at it. The obvious advantage to this - apart from the profit - is that nobody can deny that your monster really existed. But what if you see it out at sea with no means of proof? Such a thing happened in September, 1948, when the fishing boat *Ivy* set out at daybreak from Hoylake on a routine expedition. Its three crew members, Messrs Jones, Baker and Leatherbarrow, were all experienced fishermen who knew the sea *from the bottom up* as the saying had it. However, these no-nonsense men returned to port that evening full of excitement: they had, they said, seen a sea-monster - a creature with a long, slender neck, a rounded head and a horse's eyes and nostrils. Soon, the snugs of *the Plasterers Arms, the Punchbowl* and *the Lighthouse* were fizzing with gossip and speculation. Then, as the days passed, excitement turned to scepticism and ridicule and the *Hoylake Monster* became a local joke. But Norman Ellison, who knew the skipper, Harry Jones, and considered him one of the most reliable of the local fishermen, was not so sure. He called on Jones and wrote down the illiterate man's account:

"On 26th September, 1948, at 7.20 a.m., whilst about 8 miles NW of Hilbre...we all saw an object about 30 yards away, which at first we thought was possibly an upturned dinghy, or a moored mine. This object was oval in shape, about 4ft. 6ins., visible above the water. The highest part of the curved back would be about 6ins. above the water. Running down the centre of the back was a raised fin, about 2ins. high, notched in ridges, the full length visible. On either side of it, and about 15ins. distant, were parallel fins, raised but not notched. They reminded me of bilge keels. The colour was a brownish black. We then saw a long slender neck, slightly tapering to the head, rise out of the water straight up to a height of about 2ft. The diameter of the neck at the bottom would be about 10ins. and it tapered off until it met the head, to a diameter of about 8ins. The colour of the neck and head was the same brownish black as the back, with the exception of the throat downwards, which was dirty white. The head was a roundish oval; the eye reminded me of a horse's eye, the nostrils also like those of a horse, and although it did not open it, we could see its mouth...It passed within ten yards of us, taking not the least notice of us, and we had it in sight for probably ten minutes...I have been fishing the Irish Sea and Liverpool Bay from Hoylake for more than forty years, and I have never seen anything like this before..."

Leatherbacks have been cruising over on the Gulf Stream for centuries.

85

Ellison had no difficulty in identifying the monster as a leatherback turtle (only the sixth sighting in British waters in the previous 80 years) and Harry Jones was the butt of jokes no more. The leatherback is by far the biggest of the marine turtles and one of the largest reptiles in the world: adults can grow to two metres long. Along its carapace from front to back run seven raised ridges and it was three of these, showing above water, that Jones interpreted as *parallel fins*. The Hoylake Monster was hatched on a beach somewhere in Central America or the Caribbean. Its appearance off Hilbre was no accident, however, for leatherbacks have been cruising over on the Gulf Stream for centuries. They make the long, lonely journey as individuals, attracted by the jellyfish that abound in our seas in late summer and autumn. It's a formidable voyage, but these turtles have stamina; they can swim 30km a day and keep it up for weeks. Moreover, they can live happily in our chillier waters because, unlike other reptiles, they can generate some of their own body heat. Therefore, although a tropical species, the leatherback turtle is accepted as a member of the British fauna. When they arrive around our coasts, many choke on discarded plastic bags which, underwater, look much like jellyfish. Others get drowned in nets, are sliced up by propellors or end up stranded on beaches. Today, there may be only 40,000 left in the world. Let's hope that the Hoylake Monster avoided all these perils and returned to warmer seas. Jones, by the way, had a chance to retell the story when, a few years later, he was asked to record his yarns on a 78rpm disc.

The full list of sea-monsters that have sunbathed on the sands of the Dee and Mersey includes several types of whale - humpback, bottle-nosed, pilot, minke - along with all sorts of dolphins and porpoises and, as the sea warms up, we can expect more. These days, instead of hacking them to pieces or boiling them down, we send teams of trained volunteers to the scene to return them safely to the water. But what a pity we don't write ballads about them any more. Has even the sea lost its power to amaze us? It seems so.

Why an ash? Why a shrew?

Chapter 13

The Nosrow Tree

Rock of Ages, cleft for me,
Let me hide myself in thee...

Augustus Montague Topley 1740-78.

The tough, light wood of the ash tree is, after oak, the most useful to have about the farm. No wonder, then, that we find it planted all over the Cheshire Plain. Though it grows quickly, it is a fairly long-lived tree; some of the great spreading ashes that shade our farm buildings are well over 300 years old. Of late, I have been seeking out such trees and running my fingers over the bark, searching for any scars or lumps that might betray old incisions. Near Daresbury, for example, there are two ashes which may have been saplings when Charles Lutwidge Dodgson was growing up on that *"island farm amid seas of corn"*, just down the road. One of them appears to have had major heart surgery, to judge by the long vertical scar in a patch of exposed heartwood, while its neighbour seems to have endured several botched appendix operations. And why does this matter? The following extract from a letter to the Manchester City News, June 30th, 1883, will explain. The writer, J.F.Robinson, is reminiscing about his childhood in the Frodsham area: *"I remember well a large ash tree, which was known as the "Rock of*

Ages". It always puzzled me to know why the small ash twigs and young boughs were gathered and hung upon the shippon roof over the cows about calving time to ensure freedom from disease, and it was some time before I found out the reason. It was a shrew-ash, and for several generations it was regarded by the villagers as a tree possessing remarkable virtue, because a wretched shrew mouse had been fastened alive in an auger hole made in the stem as a living tomb...When the tree was sawn up several spots were revealed, marked by a brownish mass of decaying wood, where the harmless little animal had been thrust in by the superstitious farmers".

No doubt those farmers thought that all this made perfect sense, but my head is full of questions: Why an ash? Why a shrew? Why should the grafting of animal onto vegetable produce a tree with protective powers?

The first question, at least, is easily resolved. The ash, particularly if cleft, has been valued as a healing tree for centuries. The old Cheshire farmers both revered it and exploited it; churn staves were made of ash to protect the butter from bewitchment and the more superstitious among them would never cut one down. No, it is the live incarceration of the shrew that needs explanation. We have three species in Cheshire: the common shrew (abundant in ground vegetation almost everywhere), the pigmy shrew (more thinly spread) and the water or otter shrew (elusive, but quite common in watery places). A shrew's brief life passes by like a speeded-up film; a nervous frenzy of eating, snoozing and squabbling with neighbours (the bird-like twitter that we sometimes hear in the grass). Despite their aggression towards one another, they are, as Mr, Robinson said, quite harmless. And yet...here among my correspondence is a letter from a Hampton Heath man who takes the older view: "...*Shrews - Nosrows - are they poisonous according to my mate yes. they have yellow teeth with black tips and when another small rodent or creature is bitten they run off and curl up and die - poisoned".*

This notion that shrews (long known in Cheshire as *Nosrows* or *Nostrews*) have a fatal bite was once accepted by science. Topsell wrote, in 1607: *"It is a ravening beast, feigning itself gentle and tame, but being touched, it biteth deep, and poisoneth deadly...The shrew being cut and applied in the manner of a plaister doth effectually cure her own bites".* Topsell was wrong, but the Hampton Heath man is right, at least partly. The saliva of water shrews contains a mild toxin which works on the nervous system, causing paralysis; just enough, perhaps, to loosen the writhing coils of a worm as it is being eaten.

The following extract from a roughly contemporaneous work, Lupton's luxuriously-titled *A thousand Notable things of sundry sortes: Whereof some are wonderfull, some strange, some pleasant, divers necessary, a great sort profitable, and a great many very precious*, brings us closer to an understanding of the Rock of Ages: *"...To keep beasts safe that the blind mouse called a Shrew do nor bite them: Enclose the same mouse quick* [i.e. alive] *in chalk which when it is hard, hang the same about the neck of the beast that you would keep safe from biting; and it is most certain, that he shall not be touched nor bitten".*

Like mice, shrews are attracted by the warmth of sleeping animals so, just as the house mice got the blame for a wet mattress, the shrew was blamed for lame cattle. A young, growing ash was chosen for the honour of becoming a nosrow tree. One or more shrews were pushed into holes in the trunk and walled up with clay while magical incantations were spoken. In time, the tree would heal its own wounds and, for the rest of its life, just a touch from one of its twigs would cure any ailment in cattle. The practice was by no means confined to the country around Frodsham. Gilbert White gave a very similar account in *The Natural History of Selborne* (1776). White, though writing over a century earlier, was convinced that the shrew-ash had already died out: *"As the ceremonies necessary for such a consecration are no longer understood, all succession is at an end, and no such tree is known to subsist in the manor or hundred".* True, perhaps, in his corner of Hampshire, but not in credulous Cheshire where, as recently as 1941, we can read: *"Even today one might see these shrew-trees still bearing the scars made when cutting the hole for the imprisonment of the innocent creatures"* (Cheshire Life, April 1941). Perhaps, instead of gassing badgers to protect cattle from Bovine TB, we should simply have a *badger tree* on every farm!

If, as Topsell believed, a shrew's body can cure its own bite, might the sealed-up shrew have acted as some guardian spirit, warding off others of its own kind? There have been cases of animals walled up in buildings in a similar way. In 1894, an old thatched cottage in Hawk Street, Sandbach, built around 1590, had some alterations done to its chimney-breast. When the old daub was stripped away, the builders came face to face with a little, wizened creature. It was a rat, mummified in the clay, and preserved to the very tip of its tail. A rat to keep the rats away?

Once inside, she could eavesdrop on the family's business.

89

To protect corn, toads were sometimes buried alive in the earth, as Lupton advocated: *"If you put a toad in a new earthen pot, and the same be covered in the ground in the midst of a cornfield, there will be no hurtful tempests or storms there"*. And they had other uses: a folk tale about the mythical Cheshire wizard John o'th'Hill (aka John o' Hale Barns) tells how he got shuttance of a witch by burying a toad alive in a bottle along with an effigy of the offending lady pricked with nine pins and a horseshoe nail. I feel sure he must also have put some urine in there, for this kind of spell was intended to give the witch pain while passing water - no doubt it has not survived Victorian re-tellings of the tale. Toads, incidentally, are relatively well-equipped for incarceration. A shrew clems to death after a few hours without food but toads have been known to fast for several years before succumbing. Moreover, since they can breathe through the skin as well as the lungs, they can survive on a tiny amount of air. So long as the bottle was not airtight, John's toad could look forward to a long and inactive life.

Fletcher Moss, writing in 1913, recalled that, in his boyhood, any toads found in the house were thrown onto the fire with tongs. The reason had been forgotten by his family, but the custom lingered on. Earlier in the 19th century, however, anyone in the Kelsall Hills would have done the same and they would have told you exactly why. They had a local witch, Alice Cawley, who kept a toad as her *familiar*, it was said. It would be a simple matter for old Alice to snitter into the house in the skin of a toad. Once inside, she could eavesdrop on the family's business or perhaps carry away their nail-clippings or hair for use in casting spells. Better to be safe than sorry!

Are these superstitions now truly dead or have they simply crept underground? Mary Biddulph, writing in 1935, took the more cautious view: *"...No countryman will avow to a stranger his belief in the power of magic and charms, although his faith in them lessens not a whit. In Cheshire itself there is among farmers and farmworkers a more deeply-rooted observance of such things than can easily be credited by a townsman; and this was far stronger twenty years ago than it is today"*. Cheshire Life, May 1935.

If only those scar-faced ashes could speak!

The strangely restful sound of distant rooks came floating over the fields.

Chapter 14

Lord Crewe's Canaries

Few birds have made their mark on the landscape quite as firmly as rooks. Their colonies are enduring landmarks, particularly in winter when the clusters of nests (often called *crow orchards* in Cheshire) can be seen for miles. Naturally, they have written their name on the maps, too. Open one at random and you will find a Rookery Wood, a Rookery Farm, or a Rookery Hall before long. On the banks of the Weaver, at Whitegate (a place full of childhood memories for me), there is Rookery Pool, a lovely spot and a favourite haunt of anglers. It bears that name on a map of 1831 and the nearby rookery could easily be centuries older. Do rooks still nest there? One damp day in March 2002, having nothing better to do, I went to find out.

Pedalling down the familiar wooded driveway to Vale Royal Manor, I began to have doubts, for several reasons. Firstly, rooks have been persecuted for centuries. There was even a time when those who suffered a rook to live could find themselves in court, like poor George Amery of Barnton, summoned in 1544 *"for that he did keep and harbour crows in his grounds"*. *Crows*, in this case, means *rooks* - many country people still make no distinction between the two species. They still had a bad name in 1894, when Fletcher Moss wrote: *"The rook has increased very much* [in Cheadle]; *it does great damage to farmers and takes eggs. Like the sparrow it has no redeeming quality, for it never sings, has no beauty, and no dog will eat it"*. (Chronicles of Cheadle).

The dates of the annual pogroms against rooks in April and May used to be jotted down on every, or almost every, farmer's calendar. One method was to freeze the chicks to death before they had even left the egg. On cold, starry nights, men would go out under the nests and bang tea-trays, fire blank cartridges or light fires beneath the trees, anything to fricken the parent birds off their nests so that their eggs would go cold. The cannier farmer, however, knew that it paid him to wait for the young to be fledged, since the parent birds fed them on insect pests that he could well do without. Then, as they began to leave the nest, he would hold a rook-shoot which, like fox-hunting, often had more to do with sport than pest control. I spoke with a farmer's wife from Delamere who, in her childhood, had watched in horror as her father went out, gun over his shoulder, to take part in these purges. Few of the adult rooks would perish for, at the first shot, they would all scatter to a safe distance and then return to circle at a great height and watch the slaughter of their children from above. The *fliggers* (her word for the fledglings) having neither the nouse nor the flying skill to escape, would flusker from one branch to another. They could be picked off with a bow and arrow and, indeed, they have been. Until about 1890, bows were still being made in Warrington for that very purpose. Not all farmers joined in the fun, though. Boyd mentions one who, out of curiosity, opened the belly of a rook he had shot and found it full of *bots* (harmful grubs) and vowed never to shoot another. He was right; plagues of leatherjackets (larvae of the Daddy-long-legs) can reach biblical levels and many a farmer has been saved from ruin when the rooks winged in to feed on them. The truth is that rooks are themselves pest-controllers, but they don't work for nothing. In Britain, they are thought to consume about 15,000 tons of insect pests each year, but they also take about twice that weight of grain as their wages.

Even if the rooks of Rookery Pool had survived the shootings, they might simply have clemmed to death. The species has been in slow decline for a long time, for it needs a balanced diet of grain and creepy-crawlies which today's specialised agriculture cannot always provide.

And there was a third, more fanciful reason for pessimism. When I was a boy, I remembered an old friend of my grandmother telling me that rooks can be surprisingly fickle: *"You'll find rooks always live next door to the richest man in the village. But they dunna like change. He's not got to change his religion or his politics or they'll flit, no matter how long they've been there. They're very conservative birds, you see, set in their ways..."* and she gave me a local example of spontaneous rookery desertion which I have now forgotten. Vale Royal Manor was home to several famous Cheshire families over the centuries, but has recently become the hub of a golf club - not a good omen. And that's not all. According to C. Hole's *Traditions and Customs of Cheshire* (1937), when the master dies, it is wise to inform the rooks, otherwise they will be offended and fly off. They also need an assurance that they will be shot only by the new master and his friends - did anyone remember to do that?

Rooks have a reputation for hob-nobbing with the gentry and with good reason. In the days of the rook-shoots, private estates were a safe haven. In such places they prospered and were given jocular names, such as Lord Barrymore's Pigeons (Marbury Hall), Lord Crewe's Canaries (Crewe Hall) or Lord Egerton's Pigeons (Tatton Hall). At Capesthorne Hall, the rooks turned the sky black as they flew to roost on winter evenings. Very few of these estates survived the 20th century, however; the owners have gone and the rooks have often gone with them - not, I suspect, because of any innate conservatism but because their trees were felled. Here in Vale Royal, long before the old hall was built, stood the greatest Cistercian monastery in England but, in 1542, Henry VIII had it *"plucked down"* and the monks dispersed. As the walls came tumbling down, the wreckers would cry: *"Down with the nests and the rooks will fly!"*, no doubt aware of the belief that the souls of monks went into rooks after death.

My doubts were soon dispelled, however, as the raucous, yet strangely restful sound of distant rooks came floating over the fields. It turned out to be a small colony, a mere remnant of what must once have been a great city of rooks, but at least the thread of history had not been broken. The ancestors of these birds might have clattered into the sky and wheeled round in panic when Cromwell's men plundered the Hall that they can see from their treetops. They make no attempt to hide themselves. Unlike most birds, they build noisily and conspicuously, relying on vigilance and belligerence for safety. I watched them as they worked, snapping off twigs, repairing old nests and building new ones, all with much heckle-tempered debate. Listening to their endless parliamenting, it is easy to see why they have been credited with human qualities - even political and religious prejudices. They are like us in other ways, too: they are loosely bound together in communities; they leave for work at the same time each morning and return just as punctually - so much so that, before wrist watches were worn, labourers used to check the time by their movements. Some say that rooks even follow the same flight-paths and feed in the same fields that their ancestors favoured many generations ago. Their history has been intertwined with our own ever since the first farmers began to chop at the forests, making fields which they could forage in. We can understand their society up to a point, but they keep many secrets to themselves. In the 1970s, for instance, rooks were seen to desert apparently healthy elms where they had built their nests for years. The birds had felt a slight stiffness in branches no longer lubricated by sap and knew that their nests would no longer sway safely in the gales. No passing human would detect Dutch Elm Disease at such an early stage.

There is an interesting parallel to rook folklore which I stumbled upon while chatting to a bee-keeper from Sealand, Chester. Bees, she told me, also dislike change and must be told if their owner has died, otherwise they will either fly off or refuse to make honey. I went to the library and, among the yellowing pages of the reference section, found plenty of support for her belief. Before spouting this bee-lore, I must admit that, although it all comes from Cheshire, there is little here that has not been found, with minor variations, in almost every other English county.

According to one writer, the dead man's widow or eldest son must take the iron door key and knock on the hive three times as the funeral procession is leaving the house. Another says that the correct procedure in Cheshire is to go out at night, knock on each hive and say in a loud, clear voice: *"Your owd mester's jed, but you'll be aw reet wi't new mon"*. Some recommend turning the hives around as well, just to be on the safe side. Failure to observe these courtesies can bring swift retribution: one blacksmith found his hives empty immediately after his wife's death - all because the bees had not been kept informed. At a funeral in Acton, near Nantwich, about 1905, the bees resorted to violence - they swarmed all over the hearse, pestering the bearers and making the horses rompety and uncontrollable. Mercifully, they did not follow the mourners into the church! Here is an another example, recorded by Robert Holland in 1872: *"I met with an instance in Cheshire, a few days ago, of the popular belief that still prevails in many places that bees are affected by the death of a member of the family. I overtook an old farmer's wife who had from 15 to 20 hives of bees when I was last at her house a couple of years ago. 'Well, Mrs. Burgess,' I said, 'how have the bees done this year?' 'Ah!' she replied, 'they are all gone. When our Harriet lost her second child a many of them died. You see they were under the window where it lay; and then when Will died too; at least some of them went away and left their honey, but the rest died. I bought a hive of bees again, but they have not swarmed, and they have not done much good. Some folks pretend to say that death has nothing to do with bees; but you may depend upon it, it has. I always say that bees are very curious things.' 'Yes,' I said, 'they are very curious things'"*.

"Your owd mester's jed, but you'll be aw reet wi't new mon"

94

In fact, they are supposed to take an interest in all the family's affairs - births and marriages must be registered with them and, like rooks again, they will buzz off in disgust if the family grows quarrelsome.

Bee-keeping has a long history in Cheshire, as we can see from certain place-names: Bickley means *glade of the bee-hives*, while Bickerton means *bee-keeper's farm*. King's *Vale Royal* (1656) tells us how popular, or even universal, it used to be: *"...Likewise doth every man keep certain Hives of Bees..."* If you ever decide to keep some yourself, I can give you some tips that, according to local tradition, will ensure that you get some honey. Firstly, you must let a neighbour give you a swarm on the understanding that you will give them back if they fail to produce. Give something in exchange if you like, but never buy bees with filthy lucre - they will be disgusted. Secondly, if your bees do produce pots and pots of honey, try not to brag about it. They will overhear you and make a mental note to let you down next year. Thirdly, if your bees swarm, you must *ring* them, that is, grab any pots or pans you can find, run out of the house, and make as loud a racket as you can. This will *knit* them back together so that you can hive them again. If you overdo the knitting, so that one cluster will not leave its branch, take a bunch of nettles, dipped in sloppy manure, and hold it above them. This should drive them home on the principle that nettles, like bees, have a sting and, as the old adage has it, *two of a kind can never agree.*

Bee-lore resembles rook-lore in a couple more ways. Firstly, bees are supposed to order their affairs democratically, with a parliament and court sittings; we have Shakespeare's word on that: *"So work the honey bees, Creatures that by a rule in nature teach The act of order to a peopled kingdom, They have a king and officers of sorts; Where some, like magistrates, correct at home..."* (*King Henry V, I.II.*) Secondly, both are credited with a religious and moral sensibility. Bees, it seems, awaken from their winter torpor on Christmas Eve to hum a drowsy chorus of the *Angel's Song*. Rooks also follow the church calendar; they begin building their nests at the beginning of Lent and aim to finish by Easter. And, on Easter Sunday, they expect to see you go to church in a new set of clothes; if not, they will express their disapproval in the messy way that we have all experienced at one time or another. Bees have a similarly sanctimonious attitude to unchastity: an unmarried girl can walk through the swarm unstung only if she is a virgin.

The holiness of bees runs like a seam of gold through the Bible, the Qu'ran, the Rig Veda and both northern and classical mythology. Centuries ago, they were the messengers of the Gods, intelligent beings with a secret knowledge of their own. They travelled in the clouds, guiding dead souls to the other world. No wonder man treated them with respect. Scientific research on bees has done nothing to dispel our wonder; in fact, they seem even curiouser things than ever. Who can say what they know?

"Then th'piannet's row, Wha'abait yur'n now?"

Chapter 15

The Worst Nest in the Wood

The Sale poet Hedley Lucas, had a good eye for nature and a knowledge of local folklore. Both are shown in this poem (from his *Homage to Cheshire*) which compares the nesting abilities of two of our commonest and least popular birds:

> *"A piannet's a foo,*
> *A stick or two's enoo,"*
> *So spak a queest*
> *O'th piannet's neest,*
> *Bur a dumberdash coom,*
> *An' th'queest's were a doom,*
> *Then, th'piannet's row,*
> *Wha' abait yur'n now?*

Oh, I forgot to mention that Lucas also had an ear for his local dialect, a language that few modern Sale residents understand, so here's a short glossary:

Piannet - The magpie. *Pie* means a particoloured bird, while the suffix *annet* is a pet form of the name Agnes (*Mag*, in the standard name, means Margaret).
Foo - Fool.
Enoo - Enough.
Queest (also *queeze, queece, etc.*) - The wood pigeon. In Cheshire, this West Midland name overlaps with the more widespread *cushat*. Both derive from the Old English *cuscote* (lit. *coo-shouter*). They can both be found on the map, too: Quesse Wood in Vale Royal and Cushy Bank (a field name).
Neest - Nest.
Dumberdash - see Chapter 3.

The idea of the poem is simple: the wood pigeon mocks the magpie for taking unnecessary pains with its nest; a downpour then sweeps its own rickety structure away and the magpie has the last laugh. The first couplet is not the poet's own invention but a traditional local variant of the better-known *Tak two coos, taffy*, i.e. an attempt to put the queest's call into words. With a little imagination, it can be made to fit against two repetitions of the song. The link between the two birds, though, can be traced back to a fable which is very much older. In the Beginning, it seems, all the birds of the air looked to the magpie for help in making their nests, since its solidly-constructed dome, sturdy enough to withstand the wildest gale, was the admiration of all. The master builder agreed and gave expert tuition to each bird in turn until, at last, it lost patience and flew off. The wood pigeon, last in the queue, missed its turn. To this day, it merely picks a secluded nook in an overgrown hedge, a tree, or a clump of ivy, tosses a few sticks over it and plonks its two eggs in the middle. Looking from below, I have sometimes been able to see the white eggs through the thin lattice of twigs (the sitting bird, meanwhile, looks down with equal amusement on my own egg, visible through strands of hair). Because of its amateurish nest, the wood pigeon used to be the very symbol of laziness. There is an old Cheshire proverb about people who are all talk and no action: *"He's like the queest, always saying 'Do, Do', but everybody knows it makes the worst nest in the wood".*

A slovenly home-maker it may be, but the queest is just as successful as the piannet in raising its young, The Cheshire landscape might have been expressly designed for it: plenty of hedges and coverts for nesting and roosting, clover fields situated nearby for foraging, market gardens providing food to help it through the winter and strawberry fields for its delectation in summer. The wood pigeon is not a faddy bird; it will eat almost anything the farmer cares to put on its plate. Yet, two centuries ago, the species was comparatively scarce and confined, as its name suggests, to woodland. There, it had many enemies. The nimble pine marten was adept at sniffing out the nest and devouring both the sitting bird and its young, as was the polecat. Stoats, weasels and squirrels (yes - the pretty little red ones!) would eat nestlings and eggs. Magpies, jays, crows and jackdaws also helped themselves to eggs, while the female sparrowhawk (once known as the *pigeon-hawk*) was capable of killing the adult bird. But the most dreaded foe was the peregrine, which could easily outpace it in flight.

In the nineteenth century, however, things began to change in a way that made life for the cushat decidedly cushier. Firstly, all its enemies (since they were also the enemies of the pheasant and grouse) began to appear on the gamekeeper's gibbet. Secondly, farmers provided it with a winter larder by planting clover and root crops. The wood pigeon's strong beak, as versatile as a Swiss army knife, soon got to work, tearing off the leaves and stripping entire fields one after another. These birds can stuff a surprising amount of food in their crops. At Ashton Hayes, a wood pigeon was once found with 69 acorns packed away to tide it over any lean spells. Winter flocks, swollen by refugees from the north, grew bigger and bigger; the hordes that ransacked Cheshire in the winter of 1893-4 caused real alarm. War was declared.

After each harvest, when wood pigeons, along with stock doves and feral pigeons gleaned the stubble fields, farmers got to work. Some shot at them from a hide made of shooks at the fields edge; others built screens round tree trunks near a pond or shallow stream where the birds came to drink. Sometimes a wooden decoy would be hoisted to the top of a hedgerow tree with others placed on the ground as if feeding. But the farmers were up against a wily adversary, not easily fooled by puppet shows. In 1933, a writer in the *Chester Courant* lamented: *"The organisation of 'shoots' is the only way of killing a big lot of these robbers. I have taken part in a few, but never seen a really successful day. Something always goes wrong. The guns do not turn up as promised in*

"A stick or two's enoo!"

98

the morning, and the birds are quick enough to find a wood in which they can settle without being disturbed. Unless your party is working at least ten square miles of country, the whole lot of birds can be out of the district in ten minutes."

I was talking to a neighbour of mine about this battle of wits and he agreed that wood pigeons are among the canniest of birds. However, if I wanted a pigeon pie, he knew of a fool-proof, if unsporting, method which an old poacher from Little Neston had taught him. Find a nest in the spring and wait until the *squabs* (chicks) have hatched. Then climb the tree and simply tie the leg of one squab to a nearby branch to prevent its escape. The mother bird will feed it up for you until, when its brothers and sisters have flown, you return to claim your prize.

By the Second World War, wood pigeons had begun to make their precarious nests in parks and suburban gardens where life was even easier. Today, they are as familiar as town pigeons, parading about our parklands like Victorian ladies, smug and portly, their smooth plumage blending the colours of the evening skies. But Arnold Boyd, 60 years ago, warned us not to admire them too much: *"I like to see wood pigeons about the countryside, and welcome a pair which nest every year in my garden, but they forgot their manners when the snow fell. Brussels sprouts, curly greens, winter cabbage - all have been utterly consumed; it is as if a horde of white butterfly caterpillars had overwhelmed the plants, for nothing of the leaves is left but the bare ribs...We must forget their beauty and the 'livelier iris' that 'changes on the burnished dove' in the spring-time, and must realise that they form a fifth column which is making persistent and widespread attacks on our supplies of food and fodder. And, after all, pigeon pie can be a welcome addition to our wartime diet."* Country Diary, 12.02.40 and 26.08.42.

The piannet may be the more hated bird of the two, yet it is the queest that costs us millions of pounds in damage each year. If we must kill and eat wild birds, he is the first candidate. In the winter of 1995-6, a good crop of acorns brought an almost unimaginable flock of 20,000 to Rostherne Mere. What a banquet that could have made!

Shafts of sunlight are gleaming on pastel-coloured scales.

Chapter 16

The Secret of Rostherne Mere

"Of waters there is also great store, in manner of Lakes, which they call meres...and certain also which they call pools...and divers others wherein aboundeth all manner of Fresh Fish; Carpes, Tenches, Bremes, Roches, Daces, Trouts and Eeles, in great store."

King's *Vale Royal* (1656).

Each of the Cheshire meres, if we are to believe the old tales, has its own secret. At Combermere, they say, huge pike used to be caught at one particular corner of the lake. Nobody knew why until one day, a half-eaten human corpse was pulled out from that spot. A footman from the Abbey, suffering from unrequited love, had gone down to the mere and drowned himself. Other meres are cluttered with submerged churches or sunken bells, and populated by mermaids, water-fairies and magical fishes, none of which have ever been landed by anglers. The writer of this contribution to Cheshire Notes & Queries (1896) must have found it hard to keep a straight face: *"I was in conversation with a native* [of Styal] *a short time ago...I happened to mention Rostherne, when he asked me if I was aware that there was a mermaid in Rostherne Mere. Upon my expressing my doubt he solemnly affirmed that this was the case, and he added that at certain times this mermaid rang a bell underneath the water, and those who were near could hear the sound. Others in the village I have heard give the same opinion..."*

However, Rostherne Mere does have (if, as I fervently hope, it still survives) a secret resident. It may not attract so many tourists as *Nessie*, but it does, at least, have the virtue of being a real creature. The earliest reports of its existence come from the mid-17th century, but it has probably been swimming around down there since the last glacial ice retreated. There is just one problem: it has not been seen since 1922.

Rostherne is a lovely, secluded mere, the broadest and deepest in Cheshire (*"no bottom to it, it's that deep!"* I was once told), and it is well stocked with coarse fish. Here the pike grow fat, not only on bream, perch, roach, tench and eels, but also on another fish that pike of other meres have never tasted. It is a freshwater form of a fish that belongs to the open sea; the old Parkgate fishermen knew it well and called it a *sparling*, but its usual name is smelt.

Compared to the bream and perch that haunt these waters, the smelt is a midget, rarely growing beyond four inches in the lake, though the marine variety may be twice that length. For one so small, it can be a stout predator; its mouth opens wide to reveal strong, sickle-shaped teeth. It is a pretty fish, though; a sort of miniature salmon, its back shimmering with pastel blues, pinks, yellows and greens, ghosting out to a creamy white on its belly. The seawater smelt swims up brackish waters to spawn in the spring, but spends the rest of the year in shallow estuaries, feeding on plankton near the surface. The Mersey was once famous for its harvest of sparlings. Leigh's *Natural History of Lancashire, Cheshire, etc.* (1700) speaks of *"vast quantities of Sparlings or Smelts"* being caught at Warrington. Their presence was given away by a strong, characteristic cucumber scent which the fishermen could smell even before the net broke the surface. The fishermen of the Dee also found great shoals and took full advantage, for this is one of the most nutritious of all fishes. A Chester Corporation banquet given on New Year's Day, 1808, included, on a mind-boggling bill of fare, *4 dishes of codfish and sparlings, 4 dishes of gurnet and sparlings.* By the late 19th century, they were becoming scarce in both estuaries as, I think, they still are today.

Freshwater smelt are found in many Scandinavian lakes and rivers but, in Great Britain, Rostherne's smelt are unique. The earliest written reference to them is in Ray's *De Historia Piscium* (1686), in which he quotes information sent to him by a Knutsford man, Robert Thorley, who had eaten a few in his time: *"Ten or even twenty fish are caught at one haul of the seine. At the same time as the catches in the lake, or a little earlier, these fish are caught in the salt water below the bridge at Warrington in the River Mersey, which is tidal, seven or eight miles below the lake. Although those who buy a licence fish the lake whenever the weather is suitable, they never catch these sparlings except at this particular date".*

The next mention came in *The Art of Angling* (1740) by Richard Brookes, in which the smelt are misnamed *sprats*: *In Rotherston, or Rostern-Meer in Cheshire, there are Sprats taken annually for ten days about Easter, which are not to be distinguish'd in any manner from Sea-Sprats, being of the same Colour, Shape and Taste. Likewise at this time that they are taken in the Meer, they are also caught in the River Mersey below Warrington-Bridge, where the Tide brings up the Salt-Water, which Place is about seven or eight Miles from the Meer. But the most remarkable Circumstance relating to the Affair is this, That tho' there is a Rivulet runs thro' the meer into the river Mersey, and though there are several Weirs between the Lake and the River, yet no Sprats have ever been caught or seen between these two Places; therefore the Question is, how can they get out of the River into the Lake?...Some...suppose they were first carry'd into the Lake by an extraordinary Inundation, and have been there ever since, only, like the Char, making their Appearance at the Time of Spawning.*

Looking at the map, there does seem to be a swimmable route from the Mersey; centuries before the flour mills and weirs were built, they may have followed the Bollin, the Birkin and entered the mere from Blackburn's Brook. Another view is that the sea, which long ago lapped against the cliffs at Beeston and Peckforton, left the smelt as a parting gift before it retreated. Some of the locals still hold to a less scientific view: that an underground tunnel links the mere with the sea, which would provide a route in and out for the sparlings, not to mention the mermaid. However they may have got there, the smelt became used to the fresh water and found a good home in the lake. Brookes was wrong to say that the Rostherne smelt were identical to their marine cousins, however, for two specimens that Coward cut from the frozen surface of the lake in 1895, and sent to the British Museum, both have the delicate build and proportionally large eyes of the freshwater type. He found three more, in 1912 and 1922, but they have gone astray. They are the last official cases of smelt in the mere. In 1944, a writer in Cheshire Life implied that they had survived and were *"rarely caught by anglers"*, but offered no firm evidence. Look up smelt in a modern book about fish and, if it mentions the freshwater form at all, it will say: *"formerly found in Rostherne Mere, Cheshire"*.

Not long ago, I went to Rostherne, hoping to catch a glimpse of a visiting bitterbump that somebody had seen in the reed beds. I was out of luck, but, while snooping around the mere with my binoculars, I met a man who spent a lot of his spare time on the reserve. He told me that scientists had been netting fish at the surface as part of their ongoing research into the mere's ecology. They had found all the species that one would expect, but no smelt. But it is difficult to understand why they should all die out, unless the pike and the cormorants, between them, have polished them all off. I would love to believe that somewhere in that vast mere, shafts of sunlight are reaching deep into the water and glinting on pastel-coloured scales, but I fear that the mermaid has already rung the knell of Rostherne's smelt.

How on earth did domestic chicks get into a magpie's nest?

Chapter 17

The Devil's Own Bird

"Well Bob, wheer'st bin this journey?"
"Oh, up atop o' dine yonder, miles endy-wees, at Bog o' Mirollies, wheer cats
  kittlen magpies."

T. Darlington, *Folk-speech of South Cheshire* (1887).

One May morning, about 1850, a Handforth farmer was walking alongside a hedgerow when he heard the familiar sound of newborn chicks coming from above his head. He looked up. The sound was coming from a bird's nest in a fork of an old tree. It was a big, bulky structure, sturdily built of thorny twigs cemented with mud and topped with a domed roof. Only one bird, he knew, made its nest with such thoroughness: the magpie, a bird he was not so fond of. He had shot many a few in his time, because he had poultry running freely. Magpies were believed, probably rightly, to pilfer hens' eggs, but he had always assumed that they *ate* them; this couple appeared to have gone in for adoption! He sent for a boy who went up on a ladder and took the fosterlings into care. How on earth did domestic chicks get into a magpie's nest? The answer is simple enough but, to understand it fully, we must first look at the magpie's place in mythology.

At one time, magpies were admired for their courage. Even crows, over twice their weight, think twice before taking them on. Whether alone or in gangs, they have enough spirit, alert intelligence and sheer belligerence to cob their rivals most of the time. Magpies are well hard, magpies are. Today, however, they are probably the most reviled birds in Britain, regarded as little more than prancing, flamboyant thugs. We yell out in impotent rage as they guzzle songbirds' eggs or slat the poor nestlings down on our lawns in broad daylight. *"Enough is enough,"* we say, *"it's time for a cull!"* But the magpie has seen all this before; it has been called *the Devil's Own Bird* for centuries. Its smart, parti-coloured plumage is part of the problem. Both the standard name *magpie* and its Cheshire equivalent *pieannot* (pronounced *pie-a-nut)* contain the word *pie*, referring to its mixed colours. Some of our ancestors thought it was a bastard bird, born of the unnatural union of a raven and a white dove, and could therefore never be baptised. Others dated its plumage from Christ's crucifixion, when it refused to go into full mourning like others of its tribe. Its voice, too, was against it. Like the jay, it has a wide and varied repertoire of calls, from the rackussing *chack-ack-ack* to softer chunnerings and cussings. Cheshire dialect has the word *magging*, meaning to chatter or scold like a magpie and we have old sayings like *"You're making a row like a neest o' pieannots!"*. Many of its utterances have a startlingly human sound and, in captivity, they can become accomplished mimics. Birds with this facility were said to have a drop of the Devil's blood in them, so the magpie was damned and double-damned.

The barn owl, as we have seen, is a messenger of death, but the magpie has been seen as a harbinger of hellfire itself. There is a folk-tale about John o'th Hill (he who buried the live toad in Chapter 13) which makes this clear. The wizard asked that his heart be cut out after his death and hung in a tree outside his front door. A watch was to be kept, and if a crow came first to peck at the meat, they would know that his soul had gone to heaven. If, on the other hand, it was a magpie...

How, then, should we protect our souls against these fallen angels? That, as everybody knows, depends on how many there are. In the days when such rhymes were learnt in the cradle, different districts had their own variants which often contradicted one another. Most Cheshire versions, however, begin: *One for Sorrow, Two for Mirth, Three for a Wedding, Four for a Birth,* before going their separate ways. To prevent the solo magpie from bringing us sorrow, we must perform a ritual exorcism. The instructions are varied, using different combinations of spitting, whistling, turning around three times, drawing a cross in the ground (as a magic barrier) and shouting *"Devil, I defy thee!"* in a confident voice. Some advocate two-faced flattery: a Chester child once advised me to salute every magpie I saw and I know other people who bow low to one while furtively looking out for a second. George Jesse of Henbury recorded this version back in 1873: *"'When I was a young girl,' said my informant, 'if I saw a magpie I instantly spat on the ground, and then immediately made a cross with the foot to cross the bad luck away for the day. If I saw two magpies at once I looked on them as good luck. If three together, we always said three for a wedding. If four together, four for a burial'"*. Even Christmas carols might be employed, as Fletcher Moss recalled, a generation later: *"I have a distinct recollection of seeing on a Christmas morning long ago a magpie on the very top of the lofty Timothy Moss pear-tree that still stands near to our lodge. We all defied her, and spat, and carolled, and fetched her down quickly".* The carol (which, I imagine, went to the tune of *I Saw Three Ships*) ran:

> *The magpie sat on the pear-tree top,*
> *The pear-tree top, the pear-tree top,*
> *The magpie sat on the pear-tree top*
> *On Christmas Day in the morning.*

> *I'll lay her a crown, I'll fetch her down,*
> *I'll fetch her down, I'll fetch her down, etc.*

Spitting on the ground is not a meaningless gesture for, in the old magic, spittle represents life force; it gives protection, removes curses and reveals hidden truths.

To return to our Handforth farmer, I would love to know what he did with the chicks after bringing them home. Did he rear them alongside his own? If so, he was in for another surprise, for they would grow not into plump, red chickens, but lean, muscular gamefowl. These birds were fighting cocks, probably of the popular Derby Red breed or, perhaps, Cheshire Piles (no, not our very own form of haemorrhoids, but a variety of gamecock that had achieved fame throughout the land). Cock fighting had been outlawed a few years earlier, but every village still had its own cockpit and the pastime took another century or more to die. Indeed, as late as 1956, a tip-off led to a police raid on Cotton Edmunds Farm, near Christleton, which sent the punters scampering over the fields and hiding in the rickyard like naughty schoolboys. In all probability, it still goes on in Cheshire today.

In its heyday, however, cock-fighting was a respectable sport, enjoyed by all levels of society, and sayings like *A cock fights best on its own bonk* and *A good cock may come out of a bad bag* (now found only in Bridge's *Old Cheshire Proverbs*) were once household expressions. At the Chester Races it was a regular feature, included on the programme and advertised by the Town Crier as he paraded the city, banging a drum. The stakes could be very high so, if the battles took longer than expected, the horse-racing just had to be postponed, as happened in

The Cheshire Pile

1834. Such events drew birds from all over North Wales and Shropshire and there were regular inter-county affairs between *The Gentlemen of Cheshire* and *The Gentlemen of Lancashire.*

105

The cocks themselves were pampered like little princes, and to say that someone *lives like a fighting cock* was to say that he lives very well indeed. Dr. Bellyse of Audlem, *the King of the Cheshire Cock-fighters*, prepared his birds for twelve days before a fight, feeding them on eggs and sugar-candy water, hot bread and milk, barley, rice, butter and rhubarb. Some would even smuggle consecrated bread out of church so that their best birds might feed on the body of Christ before doing battle. Dust was swept from the altar and skittered over the cockpit floor to sanctify the bloody contest. To be victorious, a gamecock had to be fearless, ruthless, swift and pugnacious: all the qualities that we so dislike in the magpie of our gardens. So, have you guessed how those chicks came to be up in a tree? They were hatched by the sitting magpie but put there by a human cuckoo, a cock-fighting man who saw her as the ideal foster-parent. He wanted his birds to be baptised with a drop of the Devil's blood. Had they not been discovered, they would have remained there until fledged, then been claimed by their owner to grow up into little Mike Tysons. Bizarre though it sounds, it was not unusual in that era; Moss was aware of the practice and it has been recorded from the continent also.

In 1850, magpies were almost as abundant in Cheshire as they are now, but over the next half-century they went into partial eclipse. Coward wrote in 1922: *"The magpie is rare in certain areas, but it makes up by overabundance where the gamekeeper holds no sway; there the lesser fowl suffer from its keen eye and wicked beak"*. The gamekeepers were, evidently, less superstitious than Cheshire farmers of the day, many of whom feared to shoot a pieannot: it would surely be avenged by the death of a cow or other animal on the farm. Those who have tried shooting magpies know what a wily foe he can be. The trick, as a retired farm worker told me, is for two men to go down the yard with guns, one of whom then returns, leaving the other. The magpies (who cannot count) will think the danger has passed and come close enough to be shot!

Today, of course, they have reconquered their old lands and become the pantomime villains of the suburban garden. We hiss when this strutting, preening bully appears on stage. *"Look behind you!"* we shout, as he stalks a songbird back to her nest, then gollops the eggs and stares back at us in defiance. How dare they behave like this? We, who banned cock-fighting a century and a half ago, feel that we have risen above our cruel hunting instincts. This is an affront to our moral standards... But we are missing the point, of course. Magpies, like all wild creatures, are neither moral nor immoral, but simply amoral. The devil's blood flows in our own veins, not theirs. See how the magpies scatter in terror at our approach! They must think we are a bad omen. Perhaps they count us and chant a rhyme of their own, something like: *One for Poison, Two for a Trap, Three for a Shooting...*

Each member was jealous of the others and kept his knowledge to himself.

Chapter 18

"That'll Learn it to be Rare!"

Somebody (I think it was L.P. Hartley) said: *"The past is a different country - they do things differently there"*. That, I suppose, is what makes it such an interesting place to explore. Open one of the dustier works on local wildlife and you find yourself in a culture far removed from our own. In, for example, *Birds of Wirral* (1874) by J.F. Brockholes, we find entries like these: *"White-tailed eagle (Haliaeetus albicilla albicilla) - I saw and shot at one, wounding it badly, some years ago at Leasowe. This bird was afterwards found dead on a neighbouring field..."*.and this: *"Pintail Duck (Dafila acuta acuta): Occasionally in winter on the Dee and marshes. In the winter of 1868-9, I shot a fine old male as it rose from a fresh water pond near Ness"*. Yes, naturalists do things very differently in the past. Happily, not everybody studied their subject through a gunsight or we might find books on art with captions like: *"'Sunflowers' by Van Gogh. I spotted this one in an art gallery in the winter of 1895-6 and managed to blast a hole in it with my 12-bore"*.

On the other hand, since many of these shot birds ended up stuffed, they are now as irresistible as ancient artefacts. A few years ago, I made a list of the most intriguing records that had come up in my researches and took it to the Natural History Unit at the Grosvenor Museum, Chester, hoping to track some of them down. An interesting feature

107

of the display in the Grosvenor is a reconstructed Victorian naturalist's study, complete with well-stocked bookshelves, a microscope, stuffed birds and a collection of butterflies. At the desk, the man himself (a tweedy-looking gentleman) sits, carefully drawing his specimens of fossils, birds' eggs and insects. The butterflies, in particular, caught my eye. Cheshire has said goodbye to about a dozen species since 1850: the small blue, silver-studded blue, wood white, large tortoiseshell, large heath, grizzled skipper and six kinds of fritillary - the Duke of Burgundy, marsh, high brown, pearl-bordered, dark green and silver-washed. All of them are here - not singly, but in rows of heartbreakingly pointless replication. What had they done wrong to end up like this, crucified one after another, like the followers of Spartacus?

As in most museums, we also find birds and animals that the Victorians shot and stuffed for posterity, including some old friends from earlier chapters: the pine marten shot on the Eaton Estate in 1891 and the Pallas's sandgrouse shot in 1863 by a Mr. Simpkins. There is a shag that was *"shot while flying around the church steeple"* at Waverton in 1912 and a white-tailed eagle (only the second ever seen in Cheshire - Mr. Brockholes shot the first) that dared to grace our skies in 1863. Visitors from Europe received similar hospitality. Our second ever little bittern (and what a tiny bitterbump he looks, next to his larger cousin!) was shot near Wallasey in 1893 by James Gibson and our first nutcracker at Vale Royal in 1860. There are even tropical birds, the most surprising being a Kermadec petrel that somebody claimed to have found dead in a field at Tarporley in 1908 and sold on Chester market four days later. This was its first appearance in the northern hemisphere, its true home being the southern oceans to the east of Australia, yet Coward was happy to add it to the British list and even exhibited

The twinkle in its glass eye warns me to notice the exact date on the label.

the bird at meetings of the Zoological Society and the British Ornithological Club. However, the more I look at that bird, the more I seem to see a smug expression and the twinkle in its glass eye warns me to take more notice of the exact date on the label: April 1st!

But this is only a tiny part of the collection. Thanks to the kindness of the curator, I was able to spend a blissful morning in the cobwebbed store room, where the debris of natural history has been piling up for 150 years or more. It is like some big, dimly-lit shoe shop, its walls lined with cardboard boxes of different sizes. All I had to do was pick a box, blow off the dust, and open it...

High on my *must-see* list was a male bearded tit, one of a pair that, I had read, was shot at Whitley Reed in 1860. At that date, reclamation of the land at Whitley was already underway, so this specimen could easily have been the very last to breed there. I opened the box expecting to find a decayed, discoloured, barely recognisable lump. Instead, I held in my hand a thing of exquisite, exotic beauty, each feather still perfectly preened. The colours - brick red, blue-grey, black and white - were as crisp and vivid as when the bird took its last breath. I half expected it to revive in the warmth of my hand and fly through the window. It would be easy to condemn Mr. Nunnerley of Congleton for taking its life, but this bird was about to lose its home forever. By shooting it and having it stuffed, he gave us this precious relic of an older, wilder Cheshire.

The same cannot be said of many of his trigger-happy contemporaries. One can gain insights into the mentality of the Victorian and Edwardian naturalists by reading the contemporary notes that accompany many of the exhibits. For example, a gannet, presented by W.H. Dobie in 1911, has the quote: *"Obtained after the gale from the meadows between Ince and Helsby. Was seen alive by Leonard Schofield: it flew about ten yards: he tried to catch it when it 'made for him', so he struck it with a stick and killed it"*. It was self-defence, Your Honour! There is a black tern, a native of Eastern Europe and Western Asia, which Mr. A. Cookson, gamekeeper at Oakmere, shot in 1893: *"Two others were seen at the same time, one of which was shot but got away wounded; the third bird left the district almost directly afterwards"*. How unsporting of it! A great northern diver, shot in 1892, has this note: *"While crossing Frodsham Marshes...I shot a great northern diver of beautiful plumage...I sent it to Mr. Hutchinson, naturalist, 48, Frodsham St., Chester, to be stuffed...The bird, which I now have at home, looks remarkably well"*. Good to know that it still had rosy cheeks after being shot and stuffed! A remarkable albino blackbird has the note: *"This beautiful bird was shot by Mr, Hyslop in my father's garden (at Ince) where it had been many times"*. Perhaps they enjoyed the live bird at first but, after a time, boredom set in, so Mr. Hyslop was sent for. A pure white house sparrow that enlivened a garden in Dee Banks, Chester, in 1908 got a similar reception. Perhaps it was not boredom so much as an urge to preserve the experience for all time. For example, imagine the wonder of opening your curtains one morning and seeing a black grouse strutting its stuff on the lawn outside. That is just what happened to one Mr. Ledsham of Green Lane, Boughton in 1892. **Bang!**

Can we find any excuses for these people? Well, they certainly did not have the excellent field-guides that we use today. Perhaps, in some cases, the only way to identify a distant bird was to bring it closer. *What's shot is history; what's missed is mystery*, they used to say. It was all very different when, a few years ago, a North American dark-eyed junco spent a few days in a small Chester garden. Twitchers piled in to gawp at it and the wretched 76-year-old householder (not a birdwatcher himself), had to skulk in his kitchen until the madness had subsided. Anyone turning up with a gun would have been torn limb from limb by the crowd (quietly, of course, so as not to disturb the bird).

In search of excuses, I returned to the library to find out more about the earliest naturalists. The first surprise was that the study of natural history in Cheshire goes back at least 200 years. I have traced local entomologists, for example, who were collecting specimens while Gilbert White, the *founding father of natural history* was still alive. The second surprise was that they bore little resemblance to our tweedy friend in the museum. Most turn out to have been working men from the industrial towns (especially Manchester), enthusiastic amateurs who devoted their precious leisure hours to study in the field. Cheshire, being close to large population centres, was a favourite hunting ground. This led to a myth that the county was one of the richest in the country for plants and insects; in fact, it was simply better recorded.

In the late 18th and 19th centuries, these hard-working, self-taught men built up a storehouse of local knowledge. Many were illiterate before they began to study and the earlier ones, moreover, had only Sunday for field-work as Saturday was then still a working day. One of the most celebrated was Jethro Tinker, who was born in 1788. He was a hand-loom weaver by trade, but his vast knowledge earned him the title *The Linnaeus of Stalybridge* and his advice was sought by natural history societies for forty years. His collection of insect specimens, much of it from Staley Brushes, a clough wood near his home, is now housed in the local museum, while the town park honours him with a monument. These enthusiasts formed small societies which met up in pubs to arrange field trips or compare specimens and notes. Over time, their collections grew to be more and more impressive. Some also collected birds' eggs while others taught themselves the art of taxidermy and stuffed birds and animals. But, from a scientific point of view, there was a problem - one which gives us an insight into the old bird-shooting question. Most of the collectors were as jealous and competitive as schoolboys. Many would not label their specimens for fear that a rival would go to the same location and bag the same species. In his youth, T.A.Coward met some of the old-timers and gave an affectionate account in his *Bird Haunts and Nature Memories* (1922): *"...There are today many small local natural history societies in the Lancashire, Yorkshire and Cheshire manufacturing towns, and some, though not so many as formerly, hold their meetings and have their "museums" in public houses. I have drunk bad beer and eaten potatoes roasted in their jackets in order to attend these meetings, and, frankly, have enjoyed myself, though the dialect, to a southerner, would have been a foreign language. Many societies have a much better tone and more scientific ideals; they are led by men who love nature for nature's sake, and care about their collections as means of increasing knowledge. The pity is that the records of the older clubs were badly kept or not kept at all; each member was jealous of the others, and kept his knowledge to himself..."*

There was a Manchester collector who rocked the entomological world by finding an entirely new moth in about 1840. Not content with one specimen only, he had filled a whole box with them - 50 to 60 examples, while none of his rivals had even one. Nothing would induce him to tell anyone where they had been found. Unfortunately, he later slid into alcoholism and left the moths for pawn at his local pub. The landlady thought the *flies* were of no value and *"stuck the box behind the fire"*. *Oecophora woodiella (Curtis)* has not been seen since. One crumb of comfort: he had previously sold three of them for the price of a drink and these are now in three different museums.

Whatever their shortcomings, these working-class naturalists were driven by a true love of nature and their dedication was second to none. Take, for example, *Old Joe*, a Manchester man that Coward got to know. He specialised in beetles and used to go far afield to find new species. Their was no cheap public transport in his younger days (the 1850s), so, after finishing work on a Saturday, he would get his nets and boxes together, tie his bagging up in a handkerchief, and tramp the thirty-odd miles to Delamere Forest. After hunting beetles till nightfall, he would sleep in the bracken and rise with the lark to spend the whole of Sunday in the same way. Only when darkness came did he begin the long journey home, arriving just in time to start work the next day, weary and footsore but with his pockets full of treasures. Joe's excursions had to end when an accident robbed him of one leg, but his enthusiasm lasted until his dying day.

The next couple of generations had things a little easier, as railways and the introduction of the Saturday half-holiday opened up new possibilities. By the end of the 19th century, many were attending science classes and a few even owned books and microscopes - things their fathers and grandfathers could not have afforded. More importantly, the urge to collect was giving way to less possessive forms of study; proper records were kept and their knowledge shared. At the same time, there was a new sense of anxiety which we still feel today. If the following cry from the heart of a Stockport nature-lover in 1901 sounds strikingly modern, remember that the urban population of Cheshire had risen by about 50% since Brockholes shot his eagle, and nowhere were the changes more traumatic than in the towns clustered around Manchester: *"About twenty-five years ago...where Hardcastle Road now is, it was no uncommon sight on an early summer's morning to see stoats foraging underneath the fences in search of their prey...partridges were plentifully scattered about the Adswood meadows...and the screech of the owl was no uncommon sound to hear if one happened to be passing late at night along what is now known as Dale Street. Waterhens and snipe were plentiful in and about the marlpits on the Adswood farms and fine trout used to be the attraction which lured boys to the Ladybrook. In a secluded copse about a mile to the south-west of Gatley he* [the author] *has heard the nightingale...These recollections of twenty-five years ago present a striking contrast to the actual state of things existing in this district today - a contrast which is not pleasant for the naturalist to contemplate..."*

Cheshire Notes & Queries, (1901).

Many, today, would argue that this kind of habitat loss is the only significant factor in the gradual decline of wildlife and that we should even thank the old collectors for saving a few skins for us to gawp at in museums. But who do you think our Stockport friend blames? - *"...the townie with the ten shilling gun licence!"* Someone like J.F. Brockholes, perhaps? He should have been shot for robbing the nation of that white-tailed eagle that he was so proud to have bagged. The last truly British individual died in 1916.

In the early 20th century, the conservation movement really got moving and Cheshire, in particular, produced a series of great professional naturalists who grew into national as well as local figures. The most celebrated of these, Tom Coward, was a nephew of Joseph Sidebottom, one of the great amateurs, but his modern views on conservation were a century ahead of the previous generation. Coward campaigned for the legal protection of birds all his life and, after his death, two nature reserves were established as a memorial to him: Marbury Reed Beds and Cotteril Clough (both now managed by Cheshire Wildlife Trust). His lifetime spanned the transition from obsessive collection to conservation and he probably felt equally at home whether lecturing to university students or eating jacket potatoes with the last of the butterfly-killers. However, many of those old working-men who entertained him at their meetings never did understand his strange new philosophy:

"When we were parting from one old collector, he asked:'Do you collect birds?' 'No.'
'Do you stuff them?' 'No.'
We explained that we wanted to get records, to write about them. He looked at us with pity. 'Come any Sunday [i.e. to a meeting of his society]*; you'll meet lots of **practical** men here.'"*

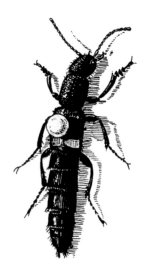

Billy had all the flocks to himself.

Chapter 19

Billy th'Duck

Today, the sandstone headland at Burton Point stands amid a green sea of marsh vegetation, dotted with grazing sheep, but the gaping hollows around its base tell us that it was not always so. They were licked out by the tides that washed up here only a century ago when geese could be shot from the walls of Burton Manor or Shotwick churchyard. On the hill above stands a farmhouse built of the same warm stone. Here the RSPB now has its local headquarters, but once it was home to a man who made his living by shooting the birds that the society now struggles to protect. He was the first, and the greatest of the Dee punt-gunners and his fame spread until he was known throughout Wirral as *Billy th'Duck*.

Napoleon was still living when the young William Kemp decided to give up his home, near Boston, Lincolnshire, and seek his fortune on the west coast. Like his father before him, he was bred to wildfowling, but the draining of the fens had left him with little to shoot. With his wife Jane, his punt and the 70-pound, muzzle-loading gun, he migrated to the Dee estuary (largely by waterways) and set up home at Ness. To imagine the view that met the pioneer's gaze, we must blot out the steelworks, papermill, the railway and the sheep, and picture a wild, uncluttered estuary of glistening mud and reflecting water.

113

The writer T.S. Birch Reynardson described the scene in his *Sports and Anecdotes of Bygone Days* (1887): *"This tract of land with short grass on it is not always entirely covered unless the tides are pretty high. Parts of it remain above water, and on these the geese delight to feed at night when they separate into small flocks...As a rule small flocks used to arrive about the 7th October, stay a few days, and then disappear for a time. They then returned in great numbers, and it was computed that there were a thousand pounds worth of barnacles when they had returned with those friends that they had, no doubt, gone to fetch...*[barnacle geese were then fetching half a crown - less than 13p - on Chester market - work it out yourself!] *...There they used to sit, never within half a mile of the shore, in a huge blue-looking mass that covered acres of ground. The friend's house that I used to stay at was nearly a mile from the edge of the marsh, and many is the time that, whilst sitting at breakfast, we have heard the roar of their wings as they rose up together. They would fly in a string fully a mile long to some other and more distant part of the marsh".*

Barnacles are the most romantic of our geese, breeding far away in the north of Greenland, so far, in fact, that our ancestors had trouble explaining their existence. They get their very name from the old myth that they were born out of barnacles attached to ships' timbers. John Gerard claimed to have seen it with his own eyes: *"...the first thing that appeareth is the foresaid lace or string; next come the legs of the bird hanging out, and as it groweth greater it openeth the shell by degrees, till at length it is all come forth, and hangeth onely by the bill: in short space after it commeth to full maturitie, and falleth into the sea, where it gathereth feathers, and groweth to a fowle..".*

Historie of Plants (1597)

Not that Billy cared where they came from! Since there was, then, no wildfowling tradition in Wirral, he had the flocks all to himself. The flat, low-sided boat that he had built for himself was intended for fenland ditches, not the serious waters of an estuary, but that did not stop him bagging as many as 30 geese in a night's shooting. Duck were just as plentiful; from the end of summer the wintering flocks would splash down one after another. In early September, the first flocks of wigeon, the favourite of the wildfowlers, would whistle in to join the resident mallard. All night they would feed on the saltmarsh, dabbling in the dark water, mewing softly like kittens. A week or so later, great bobbing flotillas of pintail came in on the highest tides to feed on the sea-blite. Foreign mallard came to swell the native flocks and the little teal, shooting in like bullets from a gun. At last, as the shoreline trees began to turn gold, the first skein of barnacle geese would splash down in the morning mist. On moonlit nights, when they had come upriver to feed, Billy would seize his chance. Lying full-length in the punt, he would glide silently out of the shadow of the trees until he was within range. Then, gently parting the rush-covered screens that kept him hidden, he would wait for the racket as the first birds flew up in alarm, then send half a pound of lead into the flock.

Daily practice gave him a subtle understanding of the ways of wildfowl. He could predict where the flocks would be and how they would behave at different times of day or night. Skrike of day was the best time for shooting because the ducks were tired after

114

feeding all night and so less wary. Teal were usually the first to take boggart and fly up, then mallard, next shoveler and, last of all, the wigeon. The streetwise pintail were a special challenge; their periscopic necks helped them to spot danger long before the others. Shelducks were a curse because, mingling with flocks of dozing mallard and wigeon, they would sound the alarm before the gunner could get near, and he had to be close enough to see a duck's eye or the shot would be wasted. Squally weather was preferred to fine, as the birds would neezle up into a mass, making an easier target; the old maxim: *The fouler the weather, the better the fowling* is close to the truth.

Billy used to sell his geese, ducks and waders on Chester market. Hilda Gamlin, in *Twixt Mersey and Dee* (1897), recalled buying barnacle geese there in her youth: *"...they were good to eat, and, from feeding on the short grass, there was no fishy taste about them"*. Birch Reynardson, who knew the man, left us this sketch of him: *"He was a dapper little fellow to look at, had an eye like a hawk, was as cunning as a weasel, a real sportsman in the duck and wigeon line, was a sort of amphibious animal, and was, I have no doubt, as most Lincolnshire people are supposed to be, web-footed"*.

Web-footed or not, he knew the slutchy creeks and gutters as well as any otter; he had to if he was to escape a watery grave. But Billy did more than merely survive: he prospered and became the owner of Burton Point Farm, rearing sheep the year round while fishing for salmon in summer and shooting birds in winter. His two sons became the great sheep barons of the district, grazing their flocks on the marsh and fetching them off before each high tide, but both kept up the fowling tradition. The elder son, Jim, lived at Denhall House Farm, a little way down the coast. Shortly before Jim's death in 1905, T.A. Coward came to interview him. The author's impressions were later recorded in *Bird Haunts and Nature Memories* (1922), and are worth repeating here. They reveal a type of man that belongs to the past and show us how the wildfowling life had moulded both his character and his body: *"Somewhat bent, more perhaps through much crouching in the old punt than the result of years, the old fowler was a fine, broad-shouldered, well-built man. There was penetrating keenness in his eyes, which twinkled with humour behind heavy eyebrows, though, like all men of crepuscular habits, he had a half-frown. This was not the frown of ill-humour, but a set expression of determination, indicative of the strong character of the owner. A firm, determined mouth, fully exposed by a clean-shaven upper lip; a skin tanned and wrinkled by many a keen wind and salt-laden blizzard - we have the picture of a man who had conquered nature's wild forces, had stood and withstood the bitter rigours of winter which had slain many of his weaker fellows. When we entered the cosy parlour and sat down with the family to a sumptuous repast, we saw the host in his true character, a yeoman farmer of the real Cheshire type. Courteous, kindly, with that generous nature and open-handed hospitality that marks the true gentleman, his very independence made one feel at ease. With pride he talked of the excitements of the chase; story after story, racily told, flowed from his lips"*.

One might have expected the author of *Birds of the British Isles and their Eggs* to feel less than comfortable about the slaughter, but Coward chose to look through the barrel of this argument from both ends. In his youth, he had tasted the dangers and difficulties of punt-gunning for himself, shooting duck at Shotwick, so he knew how it felt to set out on a chilly winter morning and see the duck *"come streaming down in long strings - a beautiful and exciting sight - against the first glimmer of dawn"*. Thus, he ends with a bold defence of the old man's trade: *"Those who condemn wildfowling as a massacre know nothing of the sport, nor of the avifauna of the tidal estuaries; apparently large bags obtained with the 'big gun' are trifles compared with the vast hordes of fowl which frequent the flats and saltings in winter. The shots are difficult to obtain, as often as not are not obtained, and a second shot is impossible anywhere near the first for some considerable time. The skill, knowledge, endurance, patience and pluck required to make a successful 'gunner' make wildfowling one of the best sports. It is far too arduous and dangerous for the majority; as a profession it no longer pays. When it is, as in this case it was, a means of livelihood, no one has the right to criticise; wildfowl are alike food for rich and poor"*.

By the time of that meeting, the annual flood of geese and duck had dwindled to a mere trickle. *"They can get no harbouration"*, sighed Jim. The Shotton steelworks had sprung up and its workers were already taking out 50 gun-licences a year, to say nothing of the shore-gunners of Neston and Parkgate. However, there was another factor at work. The Dee had been silting up naturally for centuries but, until the building of Burton Cop (1869-77), it made no difference to the barnacle geese which still came in their thousands. They came for their preferred food, eel-grass (*zostera marina*), a flowering plant with long, grass-like leaves that grew profusely underwater and was exposed at low tide. The Cop was the last of many projects to wall off part of the marsh and put it under the plough. It was soon punctured by a strong tide and thus it remained until it was repaired in 1916. The lands behind relapsed into saltings, but the estuary silted up all the more. Marsh plants advanced towards the sea and elbowed out the eel-grass. The flow of barnacle geese dried up even more abruptly. In 1874, J.F. Brockholes, in *The Birds of Wirral*, lamented: *"...prior to 1862, this species was very common on the Dee Marshes, now it is very scarce; sometimes a whole winter passes without any being seen"*.

Before the century was out, steam trains were charging across the reclaimed land, bringing more disturbance and more silting. Goose voices were still heard every winter, though now it was not the yapping of barnacles but the rasping honk of pinkfeet, 2,000 to 3,000 of them. They relished the coarser marsh vegetation that the barnacles would not touch. A new generation of part-time punt-gunners set out in pursuit: Will Lawton, a carpenter by trade; John Dockray, an engineer; Tom Evans, who had been quartermaster on board the *Lusitania*, and many more. Lawton used his skills to knock up an extraordinary gun of his own: the lock from a Russian musket taken at Sevastopol attached to the bell-shaped muzzle of a Chinese jingal brought back from Shanghai. Many a time the gun's recoil shot the whole contraption overboard! This crop of gunmen had a leaner time of it than their forerunners. Pinkfeet are the most boggarty of geese and to stalk them is to discover the true meaning of the phrase *wild goose chase*. The wet side of the punt has only to catch a gleam of sunlight and the sentries will give a warning honk. Then the feeding heads all pop up and the birds begin to talk amongst

116

themselves. A moment later, the whole flock is in the sky and heading across the estuary, touching down several miles away. *"It's labour lost to follow them,"* declared John Dockray in despair. One of his rivals, Len Brooke, once boasted of killing eight of these wary geese with one shot. An impressive effort for his time, but a comparison with Billy Kemp's record of 35 geese, 62 ducks and 150 waders in three consecutive shots tells us why these men needed their day jobs.

The pinkfeet used to arrive about the 10th of October each year and depart about the 20th of March. Harry Gill, a well-known Parkgate punt-gunner, used to run out of his house to wave his hat at them as soon as he heard the honking overhead, unaware that he would soon be waving them goodbye for ever. He used to wonder what they were saying to one another as they began the long haul back to their arctic breeding grounds. Perhaps they were saying: *"This is not the place our fathers and mothers knew; we will look elsewhere".*

The early 20th century brought more and more noise to the Dee: more industry, traffic, aircraft, and the army firing range. Before long, the pinkfeet had moved north to the Ribble sandbanks. Guy Farrar, who spent much of his life birdwatching on the Dee, wrote their obituary in his 1938 book *Feathered Folk of an Estuary: "Many years ago, the pinkfeet deserted the Dee for seven winters, returning on the eighth in full force; but this time, I am afraid, they will return no more in their former numbers - they have found 'a better 'ole'".* Today, when the locals say they have seen a flock of geese on the marsh, they usually mean Canada geese - feral birds, with none of the romance of the wild barnacles and pinkfeet. The punt-gunners died out in the end, their numbers, like those of all predators, controlled by the supply of prey. In 1951, the shore-gunners organised themselves into the Dee Wildfowlers' Club. Together, they enforced a close season, controlled the numbers of birds shot and finally put an end to overshooting on the estuary. Like the RSPB, they now manage part of the grazing marsh as a bird refuge.

Perhaps we are wrong to lament the clogging of the Dee's arteries. After all, if it had remained navigable, it would surely have been swallowed up by commerce and industry, like the Mersey. Instead, today's estuary, though scarred and soiled, is still beautiful. Its wintering flocks of waders (especially knot, dunlin and oystercatcher) often pass the 100,000 mark, making it a bird haven of international importance. As for wildfowl, the gatherings of sheld duck and pintail are still some of the biggest in Europe. Teal and wigeon are still common, though their flocks no longer blot out the sun as of old. And some winters, if you are very lucky, you may still see a small party of pinkfeet or white-fronted geese come honking out of a chill, grey sky to alight on the marsh to feed like the great hosts of long ago.

They thrust the snout inside and guzzle away.

Chapter 20

Let's Go Brid-neezing!

"The greatest enemies of birds are boys...Last week a gang of boys destroyed a dipper's nest - broke three eggs and drowned the one nestling that had just hatched. The dipper is rare in my part and I had watched its nest cunningly built in the wall of an old low bridge over a mountain stream. I think I prayed for that nest. But the young brutes found it. I learned that lads of ten or twelve set a boy of five to pull the nest out. They threw the nestling in a pool and watched it drown. I found its poor body. This is heartbreaking and turns the sun dark. Who denied the doctrine of original sin? All this grace and beauty and song destroyed - and oh! the plaintive cry of the mother bird. It cries to heaven. I appeal to you Cheshire folk, to farmers, to teachers in schools and to all mothers and fathers, to do what you can to bring boys to a better understanding and to a better discipline."   Sidney F. Wicks, *Cheshire Life*, 1942.

Dear me, what a tirade! How many middle-aged men, I wonder, felt a little stab of guilt as they read that passage? And yet, the source of your shame may be nothing more than an old box of birds' eggs somewhere in the loft, collected in boyhood, that you never had the heart to put in the bin. Don't worry; I am not going to arrest you on a charge of turning the sun dark. On the contrary, I want to take a look at the killing that has always been a part of rural life, so as to put the little sins of country boys into perspective.

One of my most laborious (and interesting) tasks in researching this book was to work my way through the churchwardens' accounts of about 20 Cheshire parishes, to get some idea of which wild creatures have been regarded as vermin during the last three or four centuries and how much the wardens were willing to pay to have them murdered. Take the house sparrow, for instance. They have always been a problem both for the farmer and the gardener when they descend upon the vegetables or strip a cornfield just before harvest. We find them in all the account books, their heads, tails and eggs fetching varying prices, according to the size of the problem. At West Kirby, for example, between 1784 and 1810, they managed to kill 50,412 (at 3d a dozen) and take 4,308 eggs (at 1½d a dozen). At Wrenbury, 8,496 were eradicated in the year 1786 alone. Much of this work must, surely, have been done by children, eager to earn a little pocket money. They had to be watched carefully, of course, as we can see from the Shotwick accounts for 1780: *"It is hereby agreed that only 3d a dozen shall for the future be paid for sparrows, that they shall be brought to the church on Sundays, with their bodies whole and unbroken and paid for there; and if any churchwarden shall pay for heads only at any person's house they are to pay the same out of their own pockets."* In other words, they had got wise to children claiming two payments for the head and tail of the same bird!

Many other small birds appear in the records, too. The name *maupe*, meaning bullfinch, occurs commonly, from the 17th century inwards. At Wrenbury, in 1842, their heads were fetching 3d a piece (as opposed to 3d a dozen for sparrow heads), which gives an idea of the damage they could do. Handsome they may be but, when there is no other food for them, a pair of bullfinches can strip a fruit tree of its buds in 20 minutes. It is more surprising to find names like *titmaups* and *tom-tits* (general names for the tit family) in the records. Why these tireless pest-controllers should have been on a hit-list is a mystery; they are so useful that many modern farmers go to the trouble of making nestboxes for them.

Birds of prey fetched a price, too. The Tarporley accounts, for example, offered a shilling for every dead kite in 1664, a price which steadily dropped during the next century. In the Neston accounts for 1702, we find: *" To Randal Worral's son for kites heads...6d"*. In May of that year, they got shut of 13 kites while, at nearby West Kirby, between 1754 and 1797, 213 heads were brought in at 4d each. At that time, dead ravens were fetching only 1d in Stockport and 2d in Cheadle.

Among the mammals, it was not just foxes that had a price on their heads (see Chapter 6). Polecats were hunted down in many parishes, while dead otters generally fetched a few pence more than dead foxes. In 1764, the Prestbury churchwardens announced: *"A Public Vestry holden in the Parish Church for the encouraging of Persons to destroy otters with which this parish is much infested, 5/- [25p] being paid for each"*. Prestbury was also infested with moles. In the year 1733 alone, no less than 5480 were killed (at 6d a dozen), and it's a similar story in most other parishes. Moles do the farmer such a good turn by draining the land with their tunnelling and eating insect larvae, yet, for the small sin of digging up lawns, they have been massacred for centuries.

Hedgehogs seem even less offensive than moles, yet they, too, were slaughtered by the thousand. In Bunbury, they dispatched 7,687 *urchins* during the latter half of the 17th century and, at Great Budworth, between 1699 and 1703, they killed 1002 (i.e., over 200 a year). The reasons for the persecution of hedgehogs are unusual, and worth a small digression. Firstly, they stand accused of attacking poultry and stealing their eggs. Are they guilty? Experiments carried out with captive hedgehogs have been inconclusive but, in the wild, the evidence against them is persuasive. They have been seen many times, both by country people and by scientists, slurping the eggs of ground-nesting birds such as partridges, black-headed gulls and common terns. The hedgehog first bites a hole near the broad end of the egg. Some then crush it and eat the contents whilst others prefer to thrust the snout inside and guzzle away (it has also been found, by the way, that eggs give them diarrhoea!). The reports of hedgehogs killing young birds are equally numerous and well-authenticated. In the Knutsford area, one got into a turkey coop and killed the young birds with a nip to the back of the head. Some believe that these atrocities are committed only by vagrants - hedgehogs which have no territory of their own and are therefore driven to abnormal feeding habits - which, of course, may explain why they failed to occur in experiments.

But there is another slur against its good name. In the margin of the Great Budworth accounts, for example, somebody has written: *"...plenty of hedgehogs are found in this high-wooded country, where too often they suck the kine"*. The idea of a hedgehog standing on tippy-toes to suck at a cow's teat may seem silly to us and, indeed, it was dismissed as a myth long ago. Thomas Pennant (1726-98) wrote that the hedgehog *"lies under the undeserved reproach of sucking cattle, and hurting their udders, but the smallness of its mouth renders that impossible"*. Yet, the accusation has persisted. A contributor to *Cheshire Notes and Queries* (c.1900) wrote: *"It is firmly believed that hedgehogs suck the cows' milk when they lie down at night in the fields. I do not think you could convince a Cheshire farm labourer to the contrary"*. In 1933, AW Boyd wrote in his Country Diary: *"I was just in time to save a hedgehog from being killed, because (so I was told) 'they milk the cows'. Many country people still believe this old superstition, and the 'urchants' have suffered for centuries in consequence"*.

Just to satisfy myself completely, I asked a vet, who confirmed it as an old wives' tale, on a par with cuckoos that turn into hawks and shrews with a poisonous bite. A hedgehog, he thought, might lick up milk that has dribbled from the udder, but they lack the sucking reflex needed to suck it out for themselves. And then, one day, I got talking to a woman from Tilstone Fearnall who assured me that she had *seen hedgehogs sucking cows with her own eyes!* Case re-opened!

I consulted *The Hedgehog* by Maurice Burton, which devotes four pages to this question and has some surprising conclusions. Firstly, laboratory hedgehogs have been known to maintain a two-legged stance long enough to grasp and suck a teat. Secondly, its gape stretches to 30mm, which is more than wide enough (Pennant's remark about its small mouth has been thoughtlessly repeated by writers for over 200 years). Thirdly, an experiment in which a calf-feeding teat was rigged up in the cage of a captive hedgehog found that the animal seized the teat *"as if by instinct"* and soon drained it of milk. So, all those ignorant, superstitious peasants may, for once, have been right.

There is an interesting footnote to this story. The lady from Tilstone Fearnall told me something else: all the farm workers in her area believe (though they would never admit it to an outsider) that badgers milk cows as well! We both had a good laugh at the absurdity of this one. But afterwards, I tried, without success, to think of a reason why it is impossible for a badger to suck milk from a cow. Can you?

Cheshire, with its secluded cloughs and copses, has always had plenty of badgers (and, sadly, plenty of badger-baiters), so I was surprised to find the animal described in old literature as rare, or even extinct. Egerton Leigh, in his *Cheshire Glossary*, writes: *"Bawson, or Bawsin - A badger...The dying out of the badger, for I do not suppose that a wild one now (1874) exists in Cheshire, will naturally, if it has not already done so, cause its old name to drop out of the Glossary of Cheshire Words."* I like to picture a family of *bawsons* snuffling about on his lawn at High Legh as he wrote those words!

If only the name *rat* would drop out of the language! The brown rat is still, of course, our Number One four-footed pest, leaving the grey squirrel, the rabbit, the house mouse and the field and bank voles to fight over second place. Boyd, in his *Country Diary*, related a folk-tale about rat-riddance, which goes as follows. In the mid-19th century, a Peover farm hand earned such a reputation for charming rats from one place to another that he became known as *the Pied Piper of Peover.* However, like his predecessor from Hamelin, he was a bit heckle-tempered - not a man to cross. One day, the farmer said something that got up his nose and, the next day, his farm, which until then had been clear of rats, was snyed out with them. They swarmed through the barn, stampeded through the farmhouse and tunnelled underground so that a potato hog, containing his entire crop, collapsed and was wasted.

The rise of large-scale gamekeeping in the 19th century, brought more wild creatures into the firing line. At the peak of shooting's popularity, between about 1880 and 1914, pheasants were reared artificially in coverts all over the Cheshire Plain and shot by the thousand. Any predator that might take a pheasant egg or chick was strung up on the gamekeeper's *gibbet*. In fact, the fall and rise of some of our birds and beasts of prey (e.g buzzard, polecat) coincides with the rise and fall of the gamekeeper. His enemies were the carnivores: hawks, crows, owls, polecats, stoats and weasels - many of them friends to the farmer! I well remember spending a magical winter morning at the fireside of a retired gamekeeper, listening to anecdotes from his long life and chewing over some of these contradictions. I put it to him that the barn owl, a bird traditionally found on the gibbet, never harms game birds or their eggs. On the contrary, it lives largely on field voles, one of the most pernicious pests. *"Ah, yes,"* he said, *" but the saying is: 'If it's got a hooked bill, kill it.'"* And that, apparently, was that. You can't argue with a saying.

R.E. Egerton Warburton satirised the attitude in his song *The Keeper* (1873):

> *The mousing owl he spares not, flitting through the twilight dim,*
> *The beak it wears, it is, he swears, too hook'd a one for him;*
> *In every woodland songster he suspects a secret foe,*
> *His ear no music toucheth, save the roosting pheasant's crow.*

If you want to know how thoroughly the gamekeepers did their job, take a look at some of the old bird books: *"Jay...formerly common in Wirral, but now scarce."*(I.Byerley - Fauna of Liverpool, 1856); *"...that beautiful bird, the magpie, who is becoming so rare an ornament of the landscape because of his unrelenting enemies, the 'battue-sportsmen'* "(Cheshire Notes & Queries,1900); *"The magpie, carrion crow and jay are in some districts almost extinct."* (T.A. Coward, 1910).

But the gamekeepers could not be everywhere at once so, in other parts of the county, people had a quite different impression: *"The magpie - a handsome bird, very mischievous, and rather too common; its domed nests in high trees can be seen all over the district."* (F. Moss - Chronicles of Cheadle, 1894); *"The jay defies persecution; there may be many mouldering corpses on the keeper's gibbet, but the survivors scream defiance from the thickets, eluding gun, trap and poison."* (T.A. Coward, 1922). By the time of the Second World War, only a few estates still employed gamekeepers, so the remaining pheasants were forced to make their own way in the world, many of them choosing to live in reed-beds, just as their Asian ancestors did. Meanwhile, the birds of the crow tribe had fully recovered, causing Boyd to remark, in 1942: *"Those who take off their hats to magpies go practically bare-headed."*

Not all guns are carried by gamekeepers, of course: market-gardeners and fruit-growers have grievances of their own. Moss goes on to say: *"Any birds that take fruit are ruthlessly shot down by some people, as also are any that are fit to eat...A gentleman tells me that he would shoot every blackbird in the country sooner than lose his strawberries...Hawfinch - a large finch, rather rare; there was a nest of four raised at Didsbury a few years since, but a brute shot the lot, old and young".* The brute may well have been growing peas in his garden, a food that no hawfinch can resist. Those who grow radishes, turnips and Brussels sprouts have a similar grudge against greenfinches, which pull up the young plants.

In Victorian times, a country boy's first employment was often as a *"brid-tenter"*, i.e., for a shilling a day, he was given a rattle and a bucket of stones and sent out into the fields to scare birds away from the crops. The boys' shouts evolved into a loud song:

> *Bird away! Bird away!*
> *Take a grain, leave a grain,*
> *And don't come again today!*

And the back-end of the year was known to Cheshire lads as *Chowlering Time* - the season when they had licence to stalk the fields and hedgerows, cobbing stones at any birds that dared to help themselves to spilt grain. If birds nested in inconvenient places like chimneys and church steeples, boys were sent up like chimney-sweeps and their bird-nesting skills put to good use. Consider this recollection from the *Cheshire Sheaf* (1881): *"When some fifty years younger than I am now, I used to watch with boyish interest the movements of the sable birds that then flourished in and about the crumbling and crannied walls of Chester Cathedral. The jackdaws' nests were up far away out of ordinary reach; but the increase in the population was at times so great, and the birds made such havoc in the spongy and perished stone, that a raid had each season to be made upon them to keep the colony down. Long ladders were projected at all sorts of angles, and a dozen or two eager marauders pursued their deadly mission at the mouths of the principal nests. I'm afraid I was myself at such times one of the foremost invaders of the poor birds' territory, and have gone home at night laden with the spoils of their young."*

Notice that a little guilt is mixed in with the pleasure of that reminiscence; consciences were already becoming troubled, even as early as 1881. This was also the era of the *Rat and Sparrow Clubs,* in which village children were encouraged to kill vermin from an early age. Bunbury village school, for example, formed such a club in 1914 and, in just two weeks, 70 sparrow heads and 54 rat tails were brought to school to be preserved in spirit and proudly displayed in the school hall. Unfortunately, the kids were not

...they paid the children a ha'penny for a sparrow's head or tail.

123

ornithologists, so many songbirds found their way into the jars as well. As wartime food shortages began to bite, more and more of these clubs were formed. Marton started one in 1917 and, like the Shotwick churchwardens, made the old mistake of paying the children a ha'penny for a sparrow's head *or tail*! A year later, however, it was disbanded, because the harvest of wheat was infested with bugs, and sparrows became the farmer's friends. And there, of course is the rub: vermin eat other vermin. Sparrows eat bugs, magpies kill rats, foxes kill rabbits - they cannot easily be sorted into good-guys and bad-guys.

While looking through some Chester Chronicles of that same year (1917), I came across more signs that a change of heart was in the air. In one issue, for example, there is a letter attacking a proposal by Crewe Town Council to teach children to behead sparrows, to get the payment for each head. The writer defends these, and other, birds passionately: *"To set about the wholesale destruction of birds on a casual observation of their feeding habits at a certain season of the year seems to possess as much reason as would be the case if we commenced to shoot small boys because they have occasionally been known to rob an orchard."*

And here, nearly two decades later, is a sign that boys themselves were mending their ways: *"'Let's go brid-neezing!' How often one hears this expression in the Cheshire villages when the lads are home from school for the week-end or holidays in the Spring and a few years ago it was no uncommon sight on a country walk to see the remains of birds' eggs smashed against tree trunks or on the lanes and paths, but in this district at any rate, the spread of nature teaching has reduced this wanton destruction in a large degree, and the youngsters, whilst they still purloin eggs now and then...take a keener interest in watching for the young birds to emerge."*

A.K. Lawson, *Cheshire Life* (May 1935)

Was it really, as Sidney F.Wicks thought, original sin that drove those boys to destroy the dipper's nest, or had they simply grown up in a world where slaughter was a part of everyday life? One thing is certain: children can be taught to destroy wildlife or they can be taught to respect it. The last word can go to a Wirral man who wrote to me about his boyhood in the 1920s: *"Springtime was for many boys the start of the bird nesting season. Egg collecting in the local hedgerows and woods was not even frowned upon then - in fact we made egg collecting boxes at carpentry classes in school and my box survived well into my adult life - not for egg collecting, I am happy to say, but as a receptacle for small tools."*

He would not dream of harming the swallows.

Chapter 21

God's Cock and Hen

The martin and the swallow
Is God's two scholars,
The robin and the wren
Is God's cock and hen.

This old couplet is familiar, in different guises, all over Britain. Boyd recorded this one in mid-Cheshire, but there are several other versions from around the county. Sometimes the first-named birds are *God's mate and marrow,* or *God Almighty's birds to hollow* (i.e. hallow, keep holy) and occasionally they are replaced by the *spink* (chaffinch) *and sparrow*, which are *God's bow and arrow*, but, normally, it is the same four birds: house martin, swallow, wren and robin. The meaning is clear: go ahead and massacre as many bullfinches and greenfinches as you like, but spare these four. They are God's own favourites; harm them and you risk his wrath (brid-neezing boys were told they would go to the gallows if they harmed a robin or its nest). In Cheshire, we can add a fifth bird to the list: the spotted flycatcher. Although not mentioned in any versions of the rhyme, it has long been protected by superstition, even in the days when every country boy was a *brid-neezer.* Chatting to rural people, I find that these species inspire respect to this

125

day. The son-in-law of one of my neighbours, who farms at Dunham on the Hill, lets me know when he spots his first swallow each spring, and shows the first nest to visitors with pride. He would not dream of harming them, no matter how badly they slutch up the shippon wall. Town-dwellers, by and large, are sympathetic too: an elderly neighbour of mine was delighted when a young robin fluskered into her kitchen, for it brings good luck to the whole family, she says. Another, though a keen gardener, would not enter his shed last spring until a brood of robins had fledged.

What is so special about those five birds? Three of them are summer visitors, while the other two are residents. Four rank among our commonest and best-loved birds, while the fifth, the spotted flycatcher, is now more thinly spread across the county. They have one thing in common, at least: they are all insect-eaters and, therefore, friends to the farmer and the gardener, but many other birds could make the same claim. Perhaps we can puzzle it out by looking at each bird in turn; let's start with one of the first and commonest harbingers of spring, the swallow.

It you were to ask a newly-returned swallow where, ideally, it would choose to make its mud-pie nest, it would reply: *"on the wall of the shippon on a dairy farm, please"*. Here, all its needs are met: warmth and shelter, mud (always plentiful on the Cheshire Plain) and lots of yummy insects close at hand. Like the barn owl, the swallow depends on us to provide nest-sites and has done so for a good 4,000 years. Before that, it nested in caves, an uncommon bird, restricted by the lack of suitable habitat. Today, they express their gratitude through loyalty: adult birds will return to the same shippon (or, failing that, a hen house, church porch, garden shed, garage, etc.) year after year. It would be pleasant to conclude that we are simply rewarding the swallow for returning, but that argument has a gaping hole in it: the migration of the swallow has been accepted only in comparatively recent times. Two centuries ago, even the great naturalist Gilbert White was not entirely sure that they did not *conglobulate* in soft mud through the winter. I believe there is a more superstitious reason and I call Fletcher Moss as witness. This passage comes from his *Folklore* (1898): *"I distinctly remember, above forty years since, one of the milkers showing me a gallon partly full of bloody fresh milk drawn from a cow named 'Beeston', one of the white cows with reddish necks and heads. The man said the milk was bloody because someone had taken a swallow's nest, for, he said, cows always gave bloody milk if the swallows' nests were 'ragt' (i.e. taken); and on the beam above the cow there was found the ruined swallow's nest, and there was the milk all clotted with blood, and the mischief was laid to my charge, and I felt sorrowful and guilty although I was innocent, for there was the accusation and the silent evidence against me"*.

If only the young Fletcher had known it, he could have replied that mastitis, a disease carried by flies, was the true cause. In those days, farmers used to keep their buckets clean by milking the infected cow straight onto the shippon floor which, of course, only helped the flies to spread the disease. The belief that ragging a swallow's nest caused mastitis was still around half a century ago, for it is mentioned by Boyd in his *A Country Parish* (1951). An ignorant idea, perhaps, but it makes a change to blame ourselves rather than shrews, hedgehogs and badgers.

Swallows that claim sanctuary by nesting in church porches ought, perhaps to be doubly protected, but not always. A Bidston man, writing in 1935, recalled how swallows would flit through the aisles at St. Oswald's church during Divine Service, reminding him of the passage from the psalms: *"Yea, the sparrow hath found a house, and the swallow a nest for herself, where she may lay her young, even thine altars, O Lord of Hosts, my King, and my God"*. These birds had nested in the porch of the church for as long as he could remember, yet they were pulled down at last to make it more tidy. Whether the water in the font turned bloody, he does not relate.

House martins are often mistaken for, and lumped together with, swallows, but they have a very different outlook on life. If the swallow is a country bumpkin, the house martin is a commuter! Ask one where it wants to nest and it will twitter: *"under the eaves of a nice, modern house in the suburbs"*. It finds its insect food higher in the sky than the swallow does and it will travel further to get it, so convenience is less of an issue. As soon as it arrives, a little later than the swallow, the martin begins collecting tiny pellets of mud and constructs its nest in layers, each of which must dry out before the next is added. It must be admitted that, in the case of the house martin, the old respect seems to be in decline. Some suburbanites (more tidy-minded than farmers) reward the birds' toil by tearing the nest from the eaves. Incidentally, these nests are usually well-populated by blood-sucking parasites - one was found to contain no less than 452 of them. Boyd encountered a curious belief that the bird carries these parasites for food on its long journey to and from Africa! Although, at least in Cheshire, almost all house martins nest on buildings, their friendship with man is more recent than that of the swallow. In many parts of the world, they still prefer to nest in their traditional way: on cliffs.

Our relationship with spotted flycatchers is at an even earlier stage. In many parts of Cheshire, they prefer to keep to the woodland edges and glades, nesting in crevices in the trees, as their ancestors did. Others, a little bolder perhaps, appreciate the convenience of nesting on a creeper-covered wall, hence the local name *wall robin*. When I was a boy, a spotted flycatcher nested, for several summers, a couple of feet below my bedroom window in a bit of coconut shell that my father had fixed there. The adult birds trusted us to come close and watch them as they snapped insects in mid-air. I would not have harmed them or their brood for the world.

Robins and wrens have enjoyed our hospitality for years, of course. They like to nest in sheds, or on any object that has been left in a shed, no matter how temporarily. A friend of mine once found a robin's nest in the pocket of an old duffel coat! However, the record for nesting close to man must go to the robin that, according to local tradition, raised its young in the skull of James Price, the highwayman. Price was hanged in 1796 for robbing the Warrington mailcoach and his body hung in chains at Trafford Green for 24 years. A pity to waste a good nest site! The poet Egerton Leigh wrote some punning verses on it:

127

> *"Oh! James Price deserves his fate:*
> *Naught but robbing in his pate*
> *Whilst alive and now he's dead*
> *Has still robin in his head.*
> *High he swings for robbing the mail,*
> *But his brain of Robin female*
> *Still is quite full; though out of breath,*
> *The passion e'en survives his death."*

The robin has accumulated a vast pile of folklore over the centuries and it all seems to be in his favour. He is linked not only with Christmas, but with Christ himself - did he not try to pull the thorns from Jesus's bleeding brow, getting his breast stained with blood in the process? This explains why it is lucky to see one on Good Friday. There have even been reports of robins going to church on a Sunday, as in this unbearably pious item from the *Stockport Advertiser*, Oct 13th, 1826: *"REMARKABLE FACT. On Sunday last, in the midst of divine service at Didsbury Church, just at the moment when the minister, the Rev. Mr. Gatliffe, was giving out his text, a robin flew into the church, and resting on one of the ornaments near the pulpit, remained there some time, seeming by its manner to pay every attention to the truths delivered by the clergyman. It shortly however began to warble, and the effect of its melodious music, joined with the eloquent harangue of the highly gifted preacher, ought to have been felt in order to be imagined, and may be easier imagined than described. It remained in church during the rest of the service, and seemed to join in offering in conjunction with the lords of creation, its humble mite of praise and adoration to the Creator. This is the second visit of the robin."* No doubt it dropped a little something into the collection plate, as well! A robin that nested in Oughtrington church in 1910 had, according to Geoffrey Egerton-Warburton, better manners: it sang until the sermon began, then *"took up a position on the back of a seat near the pulpit and looked up at the preacher, quite silent and apparently listening"*.

The rector of Warburton, might have been shocked to hear that the robin has equally strong pagan credentials. Some claim that the old nursery song *Who killed Cock Robin?* is a distant echo of the ancient tale of the death of Bealdor the Good, the darling of the gods, who was tragically slain with a spear of mistletoe. Every bird, animal, rock and tree fell a-sighing and a-sobbing when it heard of the young god's death. Did the robin bloody his breast as he tried to tug out the spear? Bealdor was also an important fertility symbol, which may, just *may*, explain some old traditions which connect the robin (and his wife, the wren) both with birth:

> *"He that harms the robin or the wren*
> *Will never prosper on land or sea*
> *And never be blest with children."*

- and death:

> *"Call for the Robin Redbreast and the Wren*
> *Since o'er shady groves they hover*
> *And with leaves and flowers do cover*
> *The friendless bodies of unburied men."*

from Webster's *The White Dove*, (1612).

The marriage of robin and wren as *God's Cock and Hen* is firmly established in nursery rhymes, in which the redbreast courts his lady, sometimes without success. Robins and wrens are often seen together and since, in both species, the sexes are alike, it was easy to assume that the drab wren was the female of the splendid robin - even some of our early writers on natural history were fooled! I know people who make the opposite mistake about female blackbirds, calling them *French blackbirds*, as if they were a subspecies. Both wren and robin have been given credit for flying to hell and back to bring fire for the benefit of mankind. In one fable, the wren returns home with a flame in her beak and her devoted husband immediately embraces her, getting his chest scorched red. In other stories, the fire-bringer is the swallow, who gets a burnt throat for his pains.

So, does all this folklore bring us any nearer to understanding why these birds are untouchables? Perhaps not, but I do have one more suggestion of my own. Some Birkenhead dockers have a touching regard for the grimy pigeons that nest in every available cranny of every man-made structure. Some will tell you that the souls of dead dockers are reborn in these birds to watch over their old workmates. They keep a benevolent vigil, cooing gently among themselves. Wrens and robins, too, nest close to man and, according to the fables, have a special concern for our welfare. People used to believe that they could spread gossip, a notion that we unknowingly preserve each time we say *"a little bird told me"*. Swallows, martins and flycatchers also choose our company, twittering excitedly as they bind round the house. As a child, I would not have harmed those flycatchers under my window simply because I was fascinated by birds, but perhaps, centuries ago, children were told that such birds held the souls of their great grandparents. I am encouraged in this idea by one further tradition. The house-cricket, which also sings after a fashion, is another untouchable. It goes one better than the birds by coming to the fireside itself, the spiritual centre of the household. To kill one...well, let this anecdote from *Cheshire Notes and Queries* (1898) be a warning! - *"A man was annoyed by the continuous sound at his fireside after he had ceased to work for the day; he sought the cricket and slew it with the weight of his body impressed upon the sole of his boot. A superstitious woman remarked, "There will be a death in the house soon", and ere a week passed away the husband and father was himself laid low, and the woman was strengthened in her ignorance, because there is no connection between killing a cricket and peritonitis".*

a spectral, winged shape, luminous in the headlights.

Chapter 22

The Seven Whistlers

"He the seven birds hath seen, that never part,
Seen the Seven Whistlers in their nightly rounds,
And counted them: and oftentimes will start -
For overhead are sweeping Gabriel's Hounds
Doomed, with their impious Lord, the flying Hart
To chase for ever, on aerial grounds!"

Wordsworth.

Have you ever been walking on a foggy day and been startled by unearthly yelping sounds passing over your head, as if a pack of foxhounds was running across the sky? Or perhaps, while driving at night, a spectral, winged shape, luminous in the headlights, has flapped within inches of your windscreen. At that moment, we all feel the same primitive shock. We quickly pull ourselves together with a bit of scientific reasoning, of course. The voices in the fog were probably wild geese. The flapping shape was a barn owl, the ghostly glow of its plumage enhanced by phosphorescent fungus that grows on the decayed trees where it roosts and coats its feathers. Nevertheless, it still takes a minute or two to recover our composure. The light of reason, it seems, does not illuminate our minds as much as we imagine. Norman Ellison wrote, as recently as 1964: *"To the Cheshire countryman, an owl is still an "ullet" and is regarded with a certain amount of superstitious fear. With the raven, the bat and the black cat, it is associated with witches and witchcraft. Nightjars, sometimes called the 'fern owl' - and all owls are birds of ill omen; the person who looks into an owl's nest becomes melancholy and morose for the rest of his life"* (Cheshire Life, July 1964).

The nightjar, when it bred in Cheshire, was considered the most evil bird of them all. It had the power to claim the soul of an unchristened child and to dream of one was certain to lead to illness or death. Barn owls, in the days when every parish had a pair, were shunned as well. At Bromborough Hall, for example, there was, at one time, an old hollow oak which many people would not go near for fear of the owls that had nested there for a century or more, while, at Malpas, everybody expected a death if the resident *white owls* perched on the church gates. At St. Chad's chapel, near Tushingham (a village once haunted by the ghost of a duck, incidentally - the vicar charmed it into a bottle, which they still keep firmly corked), a pair of barn owls nested for many generations. The locals used to say that, when someone was about to die, the owls always flew over to the village and circled above it, calling the departing soul home. The story was told of a pair of lovers who, as they sat in the graveyard, planning their wedding, were startled by a big white shape that drifted past them. A few months later, the newly-weds returned to Tushingham for their honeymoon, but the husband was laid low with pneumonia that same day. A week later, as he lay dying at four in the morning, a breeze stirred the curtains at his open window and an owl wafted noiselessly across the room and melted into the wall opposite. The words of his grandmother came back to him (*"They always come to call someone home to rest"*) and he breathed his last.

The superstition about the owl's nest is more difficult to explain. Folklorist Beatrice Tunstall (to whom the above tale was told) believed it herself: *"No true Cheshireman will peer into an ullet's nest. If he did, he would grow melancholy. Myself, though I have often been just outside a nest, I have always carefully refrained from looking within. It is better to be safe than sorry"*. Oh, give over, Beat! The only melancholy thing about barn owls today is their scarcity. In 1998, we had just seven breeding pairs in the whole county. Thankfully, barn owl groups came to their aid, building nestboxes and persuading farmers to leave strips of rough, vole-infested grassland for them. Within three years, the number had more than quadrupled. I have peeked into plenty of barn owl nests without any noticeable lowering of the spirits. In fact, I recommend it, if only to find the pellets that lie strewn there. Open one and you will find the bones of unfortunate field voles, wrapped up in their own fur. In Cheshire, they used to be called *owl skuds* by the better-informed and *boggart-muck* by the ignorant. Boggarts are supernatural beings that can appear in various forms - humans, horses, cows, dogs and so on. They rarely come up in conversation today but, for our grandparents, it was a different matter. Many are the tales of travellers who, returning home at night, heard the chilling skrike of a boggart (in reality, probably a barn owl), and knew that it was a foretaste of death. When such people picked up an owl pellet and saw the tiny skulls and delicate bones, the explanation was obvious: it was the turd of a boggart which had been eating fairies!

I have asked around to see if the death-omens still work on the imagination, but find people much more reticent than when they are, for example, giving me weather lore. So far, I have heard only three examples from the living: A frog hopping into the house, a bat flying in or clinging to the window outside and a crow or rook settling on the rooftop all mean the death of one member of the household. Perhaps the animal or bird is waiting to take away the soul of the dying person. Boyd relates that a crow that perched on a tree by a cottage for three days was thought to foretell the death of the old woman who lay ill there and, sure enough, she went *over the broo* on the third day.

Why should crows be death-messengers? Perhaps because, like rooks and pigeons, they might contain dead human souls. When the Cheshire prophet Robert Nixon predicted: *"A crow shall sit on the Headless Cross in the forest so gray"*, readers of the time would understand its baleful meaning, and perhaps speculate on whose soul would be inside the crow. In Frodsham, they say, a vicar was once told by a parishioner of a suicide's ghost which haunted what is now Castle Park. He banished it into the body of a crow which was later killed and buried under one of the paths at night. There is a similar old tale about a farm near the Staffordshire border which was haunted by the ghost of a servant girl who had been killed by her mistress. The vicar of the parish exorcised the unquiet spirit by turning it into a blackbird, in which shape, I imagine, it continued to haunt the farm with its song. The same thing is said to have happened at Utkinton Hall, where the walled garden is always full of blackbird song in the summer.

Here's an old and unlikely story that used to be told around Crewe. A young sailor from Coppenhall, named Wood, was drowned in the 1914-18 war and, soon after, his grieving mother was found drowned in a horse-trough. Thereafter, a raven was often seen perching on the rim of the trough and widely believed to be Mrs Wood's ghost. One man, the local grocer, pooh-poohed this superstitious idea - his was the next waterlogged body to be hauled out of the trough. The vicar of St. Michael's called in the Bishop of Chester to exorcise the spirit, and the bird disappeared, never to be seen again.

The raven and the crow both belong to an elite club - *the Six Spies of Evil Doings* - the other members being the rook, the magpie, the jackdaw and the nightjar. These six, perhaps because they were important to the old religion, were reviled by the Christians. To our ancestors, the raven's ability to mimic speech was unnerving and deeply suspicious. They were also seen to feed on human carcasses and thereby acquire human reason and knowledge. They were the messengers of Woden, the old sky-god of the English, who, on stormy nights, used to lead dead souls across the heavens in a wild hunt. This belief lingered long into Christian times, with the Devil taking Woden's place in the hunt. The *Anglo-Saxon Chronicle,* contains an interesting entry for the year 1127 which, though it relates to the Fens rather than Cheshire, gives an idea of its persistent hold. All through Lent, in the deer-parks and woods, giant, hideous, black huntsmen were seen - 20 or 30 of them - riding black horses and black billy-goats. The monks and nightwatchmen.watched night after night as the hunt passed through with horns blowing wildly and knew that evil was afoot. Believe it or not, that frightful image stayed in the human mind until well into living memory; the cries of birds as they flew overhead, perhaps hidden by cloud or fog, became the yelps of the hounds and the blowing of horns. They were sometimes known as *Gabriel's Hounds* or *Ratchets,* a name which is not so Christian as it sounds. Gabriel is here a corruption of *gabrel,* which means, not a trumpeting angel, but a *corpse,* while ratchet is an old word for a hunting hound. In Cheshire, as in some other regions, they were also known as *The Seven Whistlers.* The hunting party rode through the night sky, led by a spectral huntsman. To glance up on a stormy night and see them meant death - travellers would fling themselves on their faces at the sound. In some version, it was the Devil, seeking lost souls, while others declared that it was a sinful squire who had hunted on the Sabbath Day, only to be condemned to hunt for all eternity.

Were it not for the startling, uncanny sound of some bird calls, the belief might have died out centuries ago. The golden plover is one of the birds whose plaintive cry, as it flew overhead, filled the hearer with dread. In Cheshire, they nest high in the eastern hills but, in the colder months, they wander in flocks all over the plain. They used to be known all over the north of England as *Wandering Jews*, from a belief that they housed the souls of men who colluded in the crucifixion of Jesus, condemned to roam the skies for ever. Guy Farrar, who spent much of his life on the Dee saltings with only bird voices for music, had his own opinion about the legend. In his *Feathered Folk of an Estuary* (1938), he compared the voices of barnacle geese to the high-pitched, frenzied yelps of terriers, hot on the scent of a rat, which makes them a possible choice for Gabriel's Ratchets, a view shared by Coward: *"...defying the storm, the wild geese fly over on strong pinion. What grand birds they are! Right in the teeth of the gale they come, yelping like a pack of hounds. Gabriel's hounds, superstitious folk call them, when they are heard at night"* (Picturesque Cheshire, 1903). If, however, we are talking about dead souls whistling through the clouds then, for Farrar, there is only one candidate - the curlew: *"Migrating curlew can often be heard passing at night, their shrill calls, echoing from the darkness overhead, sounding like the wailing of lost souls, no doubt the origin of many a legend of witches and other night-flying spectres. On a winter's night a curlew can make the most unearthly sounds on the mudflats".*

True enough, but I will not pooh-pooh the old stories too readily. There's always room for one more in the horse trough!

133

A veil had been lifted from the landscape.

Chapter 23

Sir William's Coy

I must have cycled past Decoy Farm a hundred times before its name caught my eye. The area, just south of Chester, is marked on the map as *The Lache Eyes*, an intriguing name for a plain, over-rationalized landscape of flat fields and straight ditches that march on and on until they meet the sky. But the old maps reveal that this was once an estuarine wilderness, with a few islands (or *eyes*) of saltmarsh. Looking northwards, there was nothing but lonely mudflats and seawater between here and Blacon Point. The flocks of wintering ducks and geese must have been vast, and that explains the farm's unusual name: long ago - two whole centuries before Billy th' Duck's time - there was a decoy here. I determined to find it.

Now, don't worry - this chapter is not about a search for a small wooden duck! The word decoy is from the Dutch *eendekooi,* meaning a man-made lake, ingeniously constructed to lure wildfowl to their deaths. These lakes were developed in the Low Countries around the turn of the 16th/17th centuries and soon became popular in England. At the outset, I had little idea what I was looking for, so I went to view the existing decoy at Hale on the Mersey marshes. First dug in the early 17th century, the Hale decoy was still netting over a thousand birds a year in the 1870s, but now, with a pleasant irony, it serves as a nature reserve, where ducks may feed in peace. From the outside, it appears to be nothing more than a wood of about three acres, but inside we find a lake which, seen from above, would look like a catherine wheel, because it forms a regular pentagon with five curved channels (or *pipes*) radiating from each of the angles in a clockwise direction. No doubt, you are wondering how such a contrivance worked, so I will hand you over to Daniel Defoe, who described the operation in his *A Tour Through England and Wales* (1724-6): *"The decoy ducks are first naturalized to the place, for they are hatched and bred up in the decoy ponds. When they fly abroad...they meet with others of their own kind where observing how poorly they live, how all the rivers are frozen up and the lands covered with snow, and that they are almost starved, they fail not to let them know that...the English ducks live much better than they do...By these representations, made in their own duck language (or by whatever other arts which we know not) they draw together a vast number of the fowls and, in a word, kidnap them from their own country.*

"...When the decoy men perceive they are come, and that they are gathering and increasing, they fail not to go secretly to the pond's side...where they throw over the reeds handfuls of corn, in shallow places, such where the decoy ducks are usually fed, and where they are sure to come for it, and to bring their new guests with them for their entertainment. This they do for two or three nights together, and no harm follows, 'till throwing in this bait one time in an open wide place, another time...in a narrower place; that is to say, where the trees, which hang over the water and the banks, stand nearer, and then in yet another narrower...Here the boughs are so artfully managed that a large net is spread near the tops of the trees among the branches and fastened to hoops which reach from side to side. This is so high and so wide...that the fowls do not perceive the net above them at all. Here the decoy man keeping unseen behind the hedges of reeds, which are made perfectly close, goes forward, throwing corn over the reeds into the water. The decoy ducks greedily fall upon it, and calling their foreign guests seem to tell them that they may find their words good, and how well the ducks live in England; so inviting or rather wheedling them forward, 'till by degrees they are all gotten under the arch or sweep of the net, which...imperceptibly to them, declines lower and lower, and also narrower and narrower 'till at the farther end it comes to a point like a purse... When the decoy man sees they are all within the arch of the net and so far within as not to be able to escape, on a sudden a dog which 'till then he keeps close by him, and who is perfectly taught his business, rushes from behind the reeds and jumps into the water and (terribly to them) barking as he swims. Immediately the ducks (frighted to the last degree) rise upon the wing to make their escape, but to their great surprise are beaten down again by the arched net, which is over their heads. Being then forced into the water, they necessarily swim forward, for fear of that terrible creature the dog; and thus they crowd on, 'till by degrees...they are hurried to the very farther end, where another decoy man stands ready to receive them and who takes them out alive with his hands. As for the traitors that drew the poor ducks into this snare, they are taught to rise but a little way, and so not reaching the net, they fly back to the ponds and make their escape; or else, being used to the decoy man, they go to him fearless and are taken out as the rest; but instead of being killed with them, are stroked...and fed and made much of for

135

their services".

The ever-narrowing nets were stretched over the curved pipes on hoops. Like all birds, ducks must take off into the wind - hence the need for several pipes facing different points on the compass. Surprisingly, a few details about Chester's decoy can be traced in old records. We know that it was dug in 1634 for Sir William Brereton, a man who left his mark on the city during the Civil Wars. Drummed out of Chester for supporting Cromwell, he later returned with an army to trap his Royalist enemies inside and starve them into submission. In his younger days, though, he was content to catch and kill ducks. These decoys were all the rage in the Fen country, bringing a handsome profit to their owners, so Brereton bought a stretch of saltmarsh, intending to make one of his own. After much political wrangling, he was eventually granted planning permission and a fowler from Holland was brought over to supervise the work. Not long afterwards, Brereton went to look at *eendekoois* in Holland. After visiting Gabriel Direckson of Delft, he wrote: *"His coy is seated near his own and divers other houses and the highways and navigable rivers on both sides, nearer by much than Dodleston Bridge is to my coy. His coy has five pipes as mine, but better compassed and two of them almost meet."*

A map of 1733 shows Brereton's lake clearly, as does a tithe map of the 1840s but, after being filled in with earth and ploughed over, it slipped into obscurity. Fletcher Moss, in 1895, wrongly stated that it was on the Brereton family estate at Handforth, on the other side of the county. It was Tom Coward who finally tracked it down. In 1898, he knocked on the door of the farm to see for himself. He was taken out to the field (named *Coy Meadow*), only to find that the Chester-Wrexham railway line, built over 50 years earlier, had sliced right through the lake. The remainder had been filled in with rubbish from the farm, but he was still able to trace enough of the outline to see that it had been about the same size as the decoy at Hale, which he had already seen. Only three pipes could be discerned, so he assumed that the other two were under the railway line. An old-timer from nearby Balderton told Coward what it had looked like in his boyhood: a deep pond with a mizzicky margin, surrounded by great trees. The sodden trunks of these were still to be seen, lying in ditches around the site, which in those days was still flooded by the tide.

Modern agriculture smoothed out the contours even further, so that, when Norman Ellison visited, 70 years later, it was again lost: *"Looking at the 1-inch O.S. map covering the Chester area, my eye caught the name 'Decoy Farm'...it suggested that at one time there must have been a decoy close by. If so, then all signs of it have long since vanished and I have been unable to trace its history."* Cheshire Life, Jan. 1970.

In December 1995, it was my turn to knock at the door. The present owner had no idea where the decoy had been, but did not object to me tramping over the fields in search of it. I chose a crisp, sunny afternoon with long shadows, which I hoped might pick out any telltale ridges on the ground. After an hour spent criss-crossing the level fields and squinting at them from every angle I had, at least, learnt something about intensive agriculture: it erases history as well as wildlife. As I left, a few teal sprang up from a ditch and whistled away towards the estuary. Teal! They are referred to in Brereton's own writings, along with wigeon, shovelers, *pellstarts* and *smeathes* (probably pintail and smew). Were these birds trying to give me a clue? If they were, I could not decipher it. Had I been more observant, I might have noticed a fringe of reeds that betrays a damp stretch of the railway line. I returned home to pore over the map, searching for hints in the field-shapes, but it seemed hopeless.

A few days later, a friend dropped by with some aerial photographs under his arm. First, we examined a colour picture of the area from 1993. There was a vague, dark, diamond-shaped crop mark straddling the railway line. Could that be it? Then we looked at another photograph from a 1947 survey which, though in black and white, showed details that have since been smeared away by the plough. Creeks that, a century ago, had dribbled down to the estuary, showed up as plainly as rain-streaks on a car's dusty windscreen and… *"There it is!"* The diamond had sprouted legs and was clambering across the rails like a giant scarab beetle. We had captured it at last! From this duck's-eye view we could see something that Coward had missed on the ground 90 years earlier: that all five pipes are still there, if only as shadows in the grass. Moreover, it was not the only decoy on the farm; the photograph shows another, smaller one about a quarter of a mile away. This one is shaped like a mermaid's purse, with only four pipes. It was as though a veil had been lifted from the landscape to reveal a whole chapter of its history, and I understood, at last, the passion that drives archaeologists to work for hours in wet trenches with a nothing more than a tablespoon and a toothbrush.

The two decoys (the only ones known in the old county of Cheshire) were duly added to the County Council's *Sites and Monuments Record*. On looking through Andrew Heaton's *Duck Decoys* (2001), I was surprised to find that one of them is a rarity: although the mermaid's purse shape is found in other parts of England, the only match for the five-pipe lake is Morden Decoy in Dorset, which was visited by Defoe himself.

The following summer, the ditches around the site yielded one more secret. A long drought had drained them of water, revealing half-buried chunks of wood that the mud had preserved. They were deeply pitted and uniformly grey, as if made from compressed cigarette ash. These are all that remains of the great trees that the old codger from Balderton remembered from his childhood: planted in 1634 and cut down in 1846 to make way for the modern age.

"Look - a pair of nickers!"

Chapter 24

Digs, Snigs and Peckled Poots

'Ee conna be cawd a Cheshire mon
If 'ee dosna know what bin
A dig, a snig, an' a peckled poot,
Nur Cheshire rayly him.
We mun 'owd toth' test or aw sorts
'll say bin Cheshire born an' bred
An' then yer jus' as loik
Caw 'em as is Harry, Fred.

H. V. Lucas - *Hommage to Cheshire* (1939)

I can think of no better illustration of the decline of dialect in Cheshire than this poem. It celebrates an old tradition, now long forgotten, that, to call yourself a true native of the county, you ought to know the dialect names of certain wild creatures. In some versions, a few more words were added. Egerton Leigh tells the story of a Cheshire man who, on a visit to America, was introduced to an old woman who had been born in his home county. She immediately put him to the test. *"I'll soon see if he is reet Cheshire born,"* she said. *"Tell me what a dig, a snig, a grig, a peckled poot and a piannot are."* If you have read this book from the beginning, you are sure to know two (*snig* and *piannot*) but, unless I'm seriously under-estimating your knowledge, the others are unlikely to be in your vocabulary. A *dig* is a duck, *grig* means heather and a *griggy* is a louse (it's unclear which the lady meant) while a *peckled poot* is a speckled hen (or pullet). But how uniquely Cheshire are these words? According to Joseph Wright's Dialect Dictionary, we share *dig* with Lancashire, Yorkshire and Ireland, while *snig* is understood all over the north, and in parts of the midlands and the south. Sir Izaac Walton used it in *The Compleat Angler* (1653): *"...in a warm day in Summer I have taken many a good Eel by 'sniggling' and have been much pleased with that sport".* *Grig* is a Welsh word - one of the very few that Cheshire folk have borrowed from the old enemy. The word *Peckled* has been heard in many midland counties, although the combination *peckled poot* does seem to be a Cheshire speciality. The name *piannot*, which, instead of giving the pie the name *Maggie*, christens her *Annette*, is common currency all over Scotland and the north. Dialect words, then, do not belong to particular regions or define their boundaries - they are simply words that have dropped out of standard usage but live on in everyday speech, surviving longer in some places than others. *Snig* is no more a Cheshire word than the red kite is a purely Welsh bird; both were once found across the whole country and, with more imaginative attitudes to wildlife and language, can be so again.

Here's another example of dialect's decline. When, as a boy, I began to follow local football, I could never understand why Runcorn supporters shouted *"Come on the Linnets!"* when their team plays in green and yellow. Altrincham's nickname, *The Robins*, made more sense, because their plumage - sorry, shirts - were red and white, but, surely, a team called *The Linnets* ought to play in pink shirts and white shorts, with grey caps! It was many years before I found the answer - not from a bird book, but from an old countryman...

For nearly 20 years, on and off, I have done recording work for the Cheshire Wildlife Trust. That is to say, I have spent many happy summer days wandering through woods, across meadows, around ponds and along canal banks, listing all the plants I could find, taking note of any birds, mammals or insects I saw, and posting off the information. On one memorable occasion, in the 1980s, I was at an old common, not many miles from Malpas, when an old codger emerged from his cottage to see what I was agate. He turned out to be a keen observer of wildlife, eager to tell me which birds he had seen and where they nested. I told him that I had found no true rarities, but that some of the plants, such as devil's bit, musk mallow and cowslips, were becoming scarce in the area, and he was amazed that I could get so excited about flowers that, in his boyhood, were as common as muck. He was a wiry, active man, one of that generation (now nearly extinct) that rarely took their caps off and believed that trousers should be pulled up at least as high as the ribcage. He was not in the habit of smiling, but there was warmth and humour in his smoky voice and his milky eyes were alert. Despite the trousers, I could see that he was nobody's fool; nor was he anybody's *marvellous old character.* He talked about the farm (he had spent his whole life there) and the wildlife nearby: the

139

badgers in the woods, the glow-worms on the railway line, the orchids in the mizzicky field. And, as he spoke, I found, with mingled bewilderment and delight, that I could not quite understand it all. He made free use of the old Cheshire negatives (*dunna, conna, wunna, wilna, etc*), dropped the final L in words like *wall* and *call,* turning them into *war* and *caw* and pronounced *day* and *rain* as *dee* and *reen.* It sounded strange, yet, at the same time, deeply familiar - something I had known all my life, without realising it. Leafing through my bird-guide, he told me what he was used to calling each one. He knew starlings as *shepsters*, sparrows as *spadgers*, chaffinches as *pinks,* greenfinches as *green linnets* (eureka!), pipits as *titlarks,* and so on through the whole book. At one point, I misunderstood him and, taking my confusion for mockery, he shot me a suspicious, intelligent glance, which showed that he was used to being ridiculed for speech-patterns that he was too old, or too stubborn, to change. That glance told me the true reason why people have discarded their dialect over the past century. Speak like a peasant and you will be treated like one. I was too shy to tell him that I loved the way he talked. Of course, when he was a boy, this was the everyday language of the Cheshire countryside, as common as the chattering of sparrows, but in the 1980s, it was like hearing the boom of a lonely bitterbump that had lingered on, unnoticed, into the modern era. I had found a rarity, after all.

Many Cheshire people seem quite unaware of the existence of their local dialect and, looking through the forgotten pages of Darlington's *Folk-speech of South Cheshire* (1887), I find that the attitude was the same in his day: *"The ordinary South Cheshire countryman is totally without that sense of pride in, and respect for, his own idioms, which alone makes a dialectal literature possible"*. Yet Darlington's work, with its scholarly treatment of vocabulary, grammar and pronunciation, reveals Cheshire dialect to be a rich and expressive language. Folk-speech has faded away all over Britain, to be sure, but, in Cheshire, even its memory has been erased and the words that are still used pass unnoticed, even by the speakers themselves.

My meeting with the old man inspired me to compile my own list of Cheshire's bird and animal names, gleaned both from old books and the memories of old people. The collection now numbers over 200 (some, like *shepster*, still in regular use, others, like *bitterbump*, long forgotten) and, although it may sound a lot, it is really only a remnant of our lost vocabulary. Now, I am not going to recommend that all these names be revived, for two reasons. Firstly, because birdwatchers, in my experience, are confused enough as it is. The traditional Cheshire name for a yellowhammer is *goldfinch*, while the official goldfinch is called a *nicker*, or *jack nicker.* Similarly, the name *blackcap* is shared by the stonechat and the reed bunting, both of which have black heads like the official blackcap, which has the old name of *man-of-the-woods*, a name it shares with the orang-utan. See the problem? The second reason is that local names, even more than the standard ones, tend to place birds in the wrong families. Scientists have long protested that a hedge sparrow is not a kind of sparrow, nor a long-tailed tit a kind of tit, but the names in my list reshuffle the bird families shamelessly: *saw finch* (great tit), *golden wren* (siskin), *titlark* (meadow pipit), *black martin* (swift), *pit sparrow* (sedge warbler and reed bunting) and so on. On the other hand, some of these names allow us

140

to make pleasing pairs of birds, such as redwings and *bluebacks* (fieldfares, which accompany redwings in winter) and golden plovers and *silver plovers* (grey plovers). And whereas the field guides contain only one bird called a linnet, my list has five: *brown linnet* linnet), *red linnet* (goldfinch), *green linnet* (greenfinch), *moor linnet* (twite) and *moss linnet* (dunnock or hedge sparrow).

Many old bird names show accurate observation and that, at least, makes them worthy of our memory. Take the nightjar, for instance. In Cheshire, it has been given at least eight other names, each of which tells us something about the bird: *fern owl* and *bracken owl* tell us where to find it, *evening jar* and *night hawk* indicate when it can be seen, *moth owl* tells us what it eats, *jenny spinner* what it sounds like and *goat-sucker* and *lich fowl* remind us of its sinister folklore. That last name is a speciality of the Peckforton area, and should be pronounced with a long vowel (*lie-ch*), as in the old pronunciation of Nantwich. It means *corpse bird,* which suggests that the nightjar's song was thought to bring death nearer. Perhaps, like the tapping of the deathwatch beetle, it reminded people of the death-rattle.

The long-tailed tit has names that refer to its appearance (*dogtail, long-tailed pie* and *two-fingered tit*) and others that describe its nest (*churn, bottle tit* and *Billy feather-poke*), while the whitethroat is a *smastray* (i.e., small-straw), since it uses the finest straw to build its nest. Even the eggs of a bird can inspire a folk-name - what species do you think Lenna Bickerton is referring to in this passage from her *Memories of a Cheshire Childhood?: "The lane...had scribble larks' nests in its banks. The tiny eggs appeared as though a child had doodled on their shells with a pencil and they fascinated me..."* The *scribble lark* is better known as the yellowhammer. Speckles are added to an egg just before it is laid but, in the case of the yellowhammer, the wet pigment becomes streaked as the egg twists its way down the oviduct. Other birds have names that give insights into their behaviour: the blue tit and the pied wagtail were both given the name *Billy-biter* by brid-neezing boys who found that the sitting bird would peck at their fingers; starlings are called *shepsters* (i.e. *sheep stares*) because they perch on the backs of sheep and peck out their ticks; the mistle thrush's habit of singing at full throttle, no matter how bad the weather, earned it the name *stormcock*. Some names are simply more accurate or vivid than the standard ones; I would gladly champion *copper-nob* (tree sparrow), *blue cap* (blue tit), *pied finch* (chaffinch), *gorse-hopper* (whinchat), *nettle-creeper* (whitethroat), *windhover* (a perfect description of the kestrel's flight), and *mattock* (Northwich salt miners gave that name to the swift, because its shape resembles one of their tools). And can you think of a lovelier name for the yellowhammer than *golden amber*, or, for that matter, a coarser name for the seemingly legless great crested grebe than *foot-in-arse*?. The names that describe birds by their calls are just as descriptive, e.g., *stone-breaker* (wheatear) and *razzor-grinder* (sedge warbler). Others use onomatopoeia, like *winter utick* and *little utick* (stonechat and whinchat), *pink, twink* or *spink* (chaffinch - take your choice) and *jitty* (redpoll). There is, by the way, a true story about a Cheshire bird-catcher who was caught with redpolls (protected birds) in his possession. In court, he based his defence on the fact that they were not redpolls at all, but *jitties*. The arresting officer did all he could to convince the magistrate that they are

141

one and the same, but to no avail. The case was dismissed! Redpolls, incidentally, were once favourite cage birds. Geoffrey Egerton-Warburton wrote,in 1912: *"Lesser redpoles, which here they call 'jitties'...I have heard of one boy catching 50 in a season; for these he got a few pence apiece in Warrington"*. On the other hand, there was a popular taboo against caging young birds, as Boyd noted: *"That old birds will poison their young, when taken from the nest and caged, is firmly believed. Some young song thrushes were caged at Frandley and fed by the adults, but died when just full grown. The owner had no doubt at all that they had been poisoned to prevent their being kept captive"*.

The startling cries of the swift have led to names like *devil screamer, squayler* and *squeak* and inspired H.V.Lucas to write another of his dialect poems:

> *Th' squayler's abait*
> *"Chee-ree-eee",*
> *Skei-heigh, in an' ait,*
> *Wi' kneife-loike wings.*
> *It's gud ta sey*
> *Sich dartin' things*
> *As them brids bey,*
> *A-skrikin joy.*
> *Then coom ta reest*
> *In wall or roof*
> *Or teilin's neest,*
> *Full-ballied wi' flies.*

Birds that are considered unusual are sometimes regarded as foreigners. Thus, we have names like *Scotch queece* (stock dove), *Scotch thrush* (fieldfare), *French bird* (fieldfare again), *French curlew* (curlew), *French dove* (collared dove) and *Norway crow* (hooded crow). But the most interesting names of all are those which reveal the beliefs of the people who invented them. *Sheep's guide,* a name given to the golden plover by the shepherds of Longdendale in the north-eastern tip of Cheshire, is a case in point. As I said in Chapter 22, this bird's haunting call used to be feared as one of the *Seven Whistlers,* but the shepherds thought it was a warning, telling the sheep out on the windswept moors that a dangerous human was approaching. Another example is *Jack nicker,* which puzzled the dialect collector Roger Wilbraham back in 1826: *"Jack nicker - a goldfinch: why so called I cannot conjecture"*. The reason is that the goldfinch, before the Reformation, was linked with St. Nicholas, the saint who gave bags of gold to three poor girls for their dowries, and has since been transmutated into our Santa Claus. In that era, the saint was known as *Nicol* which, given the Cheshire habit of leaving off final Ls, gives us *nicker.* Interestingly enough, my old countryman called the bird a *nickle* (pronouncing the L for once), which seems to be a previously unrecorded variant. Somehow, I can't see the name *nicker* catching on with today's birdwatchers - who wants to shout out *"Look - a pair of nickers flying past!"* ?

There is still another reason to cherish dialect names: they help us to understand old place-names. Some, such as Gleadsmoss and Marthall have been explained in earlier chapters, but there are plenty more examples. So, here's a little quiz - not to find out if you are *'reet Cheshire born'*, but to see if this book is helping you to rediscover your lost heritage. Cover up the answers and see how many of these place-names you can decipher. If you score higher than ten, you already know more than most.

1. Diglake Farm (88/64) 2. Snig Hall (71/72) 3. Pyegreave Farm (93/72) 4. Asker Meadow (a field name from Bosley) 5. Toad Hall Farm (77/53) 6. Paddockhill (81/79) 7. Urchins Kitchen (54/67) 8. Pott Shrigley (94/79) 9. Throstlegrove (94/88) 10. Lappinch Hall (60/77 - a lost place-name) 11. Queastybirch Hall (60/81)12. Ullardhall Farm (74/76)13. Hooterhall (73/58) 14. Baguley (81/89) 15. Gresty Bridge (70/53) 16. Coneygreaves Farm (60/66) 17. Rotten Row (the old name for Pepper Street in Nantwich) 18. Maw Green (71/57) 19. Rostherne (74/83) 20. Breeze Hill (56/50)

Answers. 1. A lake where ducks dabble. 2. A hall at a spot where eels may have been caught in the past. 3. A grove of trees where magpies gather. 4. A meadow with a pit where newts (or *yellow-bellied askers*) are found. In the days when Cheshire was still dotted with peat bogs and mosses (we had 28 square miles of them 200 years ago), the folk who dwelt on them were known as *yellow-bellies* - not for their cowardice, but for their supposedly amphibious lifestyle.The word *asker,* incidentally, derives from the Old English *aôexe.* However, an old woman from Northwich had another theory. Newts used to daddle into her cottage and rear up on their hind legs as if asking us for food. Perhaps, she reasoned, they are called *askers* because they *ask us.* but are they really begging for food? Topsell wrote, in 1608, that *"being moved to anger, it standeth upon the hinder legs and looketh directly in the face of him that hath stirred it"*, and that *"there is nothing in nature that so much offendeth it as salt"*. A newtthat has been hibernating in some crevice in the salty earth of Northwich must, therefore, be in a pretty radgy mood, so don't get too close - they can spit fire, you know! 5. No, nothing to do with The Wind in the Willows! Toad is here a corruption of *Tod,* which means a fox, as in the old Cheshire saying *As hard as a north toad* (as tough as a northern fox). As if to prove the point, there is a Foxley Farm nearby. 6. Paddock, on the other hand, *does* mean a toad! 7. A ravine where hedgehogs get together. 8. Shrigley, surprisingly, means a grove of mistle thrushes. This bird's old, onomatopoeic name, *shrike*, has now been usurped by the butcher bird but, since the mistle thrush has at least eleven other Cheshire names, it can spare this one. 9. The *throstle* is, of course, its cousin, the song thrush, as in the old Cheshire saying *To stare like a choked throstle* (it will sit tight on the nest and gaze back at you until you can almost touch it). Incidentally, Cheshire people used to think a thrush that laid as early as March was a different species - the *March Throstle,* whose eggs were more speckled than usual. In today's warmer climate, British birds are nesting, on average, 17 days earlier than they did 25 years ago, so most thrushes must now be March Throstles! They are lucky birds too, as Geoffrey Egerton-Warburton explains: *"A particular throstle will choose his favourite spot to sing from, and will keep to it more or less throughout the season. The point of a gable of the house is one such place (it is a Cheshire belief that a throstle brings you good luck when he chooses your house to sing from"*. 10. Of all the lapwing's names, this one (unique to

143

Cheshire) is closest to the original Old English name *laepewince*, which has nothing to do with flapping wings, but refers to the bird's bobbing crest. In Boyd's day, *Lappinch 'Aw* was often surrounded by huge flocks of lappinches and golden plover, but times have changed. 11. A grove of birches where wood pigeons gather. In this case, times have not changed - in fact, our woods are more *queasty* than ever! 12. A farm where owls abound. 13. Nothing to do with noses - this is another owly place. Another of those old Cheshire sayings goes *He's swapped his hen for a hooter* i.e. made a bad exchange. Oddly enough, Owler Farm (50/58) means a farm with alder trees, using the local pronunciation *owler* or *oller*, yet Owley Wood (62/74) really does mean a wood with owls (and I hope it still has them). 14. Baguley means badger-clearing. We also have place names like Broxton , that use the old name *brock*, but we must remember that Brock, centuries ago, could also be a man's name. 15. Gresty derives from the strange-sounding *graeg-stig,* meaning a badger-run, *grey* being another old name for the beast. There is a *Grey's Gate* (53/70) on the edge of Delamere Forest where badgers used to come and go and, no doubt, still do today. 16. Coneygreaves Farm is the site of an old rabbit warren. Rabbits, then known as conies, were introduced for food in mediaeval times and jealously guarded. Like fallow deer, they went native, although it was not until the 17th century that they became a pest. King's Vale Royal (1656) mentions a *"great store of Conies, both black and gray"* in Delamere Forest. 17. Rotten Row means a row of houses infested by *rots* (rats). 18. Maw is an old word meaning any kind of seagull, so Maw Green, before Crewe sprawled over it, may have been a marshy area where black-headed gulls bred. 19 Rostherne means a roost of herons, using the old name *hern* or *yarn*. Heronbridge (41/64), on the other hand, comes from *hyrne*, meaning a secluded nook. 20. Cows that, in summer, gallop around the field tormented by flies are still sometimes described as '*brizzin'* by the farmer. A *brizz* is a gadfly, so Breeze Hill sounds like a place to avoid on hot days.

Fifteen years after my meeting with the old man, I returned to look over the common again. It was time to update my old survey of the site, checking off the plants and taking note of any changes. The news was mostly good: the place had not been damaged, the cowslips, mallows and scabiouses were still growing there, a twittering party of *nickles* danced overhead and a *coot* (i.e. moorhen) had raised a brood on the pit. But there was one important change. He had died, and a new family had taken up residence in his cottage. Nothing wrong in that - they may, for all I know, be excellent people - but old folk like him are a living incarnation of our heritage. Their habitat - the small, settled community - has given way to the monoculture of suburbia and is now as rare in Cheshire as heathland or fen. But, while bitterns and nightjars may, one day breed with us again, the people who knew the old lore will never be replaced.

I must confess that I forgot most of the bird and plant names that he gave me on that day. I intended to go and see him again to learn all his store of nature lore and perhaps put his voice on tape, but it was easier to make excuses to myself. *"It's a long way on my bike - perhaps somebody else'll do it."* Nobody did.

The reapers rushed to flush the hare into a neighbour's field.

Chapter 25

Shutting the Hare

"The people of the Countrey, are of nature very gentle and courteous, ready to help and further one another; and that is to be seen chiefly in the Harvest time; how careful they are of one another. In Religion very zealous, howbeit somewhat addicted to Superstition, which cometh through want of Preaching. 'For the Harvest is plenty, but the Reapers are few'."

Daniel King, *The Vale Royal of England* (1656).

The Victorian folklorist Robert Holland preserved many old Cheshire proverbs, but two sayings that he claimed never to have heard in the home county of Lewis Carroll are: *To grin like a Cheshire cat* and *As mad as a March Hare*. Our traditional word for a March Hare is *wyndy*, a more precise word, meaning *wild, shattery, scatty - hare-brained*, in fact. On the other hand, the hare is an important Cheshire animal, for at least two reasons. Firstly, it's quite possible that the brown hare, which once had nicknames like *puss* and *the cat of the woods*, actually *is* the original Cheshire Cat (no, I've never seen a hare grin either, but it makes a change from the more usual theories). Secondly, whether mad or sane, it has a special place in the county's folklore, as we shall see.

Hares are mysterious animals: they live their whole lives in the open, yet we know far less about them than we do about the burrowing rabbit. They were probably introduced to these parts by the Romans as beasts of the chase and they have been on the run ever since. Despite their persecution, hares thrived in our countryside and reached peak numbers in the late Victorian era when gamekeepers, unwittingly, helped them by murdering their natural enemies. The great decline began in the 1960s, as the Cheshire Plain became transformed into the great, green food factory that we know today. Since then, the wretched leverets have been burnt along with the stubble, sprayed with paraquat and chopped up in combine harvesters. Those that survive often starve during the autumn as, after harvest, the land is ploughed up ready for the winter wheat and, until it springs up, the cupboard is bare. If the hare really is the Cheshire Cat, she has nothing to grin about. In the past, however, harvest time made her into a star...

Imagine, for a moment, that you have slipped back in time to the 1850s. It is early September, and you are travelling on horseback from Altrincham to Northwich on a still, golden evening. You are surrounded by cornfields: smaller than those of today, with neater, trimmer hedges. Many have already been harvested while others still shine in the evening sun – tawny gold, with a skittering of scarlet poppies. In some you can see teams of men rhythmically scything down the corn. They work from the edge of the field towards the middle, until only a small island of standing corn is left. It's a busy, bustling scene and everybody seems in a great hurry to get the work done. Suddenly, you hear a loud, raucous chanting from several fields away:

> *"We'n sheared and shorn,*
> *We'n sent the hare*
> *To Mester Frith's corn!*
> *Sickery sickery shorn, hip, hip, hooray!"*

You trot on past a couple more farms and once again the air is filled with wild shouts:

> *"Oh yes! Oh yes! Oh yes!*
> *This is to give notice that Mester Barber has gen the seck a turn*
> *And sent th'owd hare into Mester Hewitt's standing curn! "*

This time, you stop to watch. On a high ridge stands a cluster of men, almost silhouetted against the evening sky. They join hands, bend low, and begin to utter a strange cry, like *"wow-wow-wow!"* You come a little closer and watch from behind the hedge. Now the men are standing in a line, taking turns to throw their sickles at three stalks of corn that have been left standing and tied together with a blue ribbon. After several failed attempts, one man cuts it (to loud cheers) and they all head home, laughing and passing round jugs of beer. You stop one of them - the winner of the contest - and ask him what the strange chanting was all about. He tells you that it is called a *nominy* and it's sung at every harvest to celebrate *Shutting the Hare*. He seems quite triumphant about the fact that this hare has been driven onto Farmer Frith's land. He's a little vague about whether or not an actual hare was seen and exactly why it must be driven away, but he assures

146

you that the custom has been going on for a long time – since he were a lad, like. The mell supper is waiting, so you let him get his fitchet pie (the traditional harvester's reward, filled with bacon, onion and apple) and continue your journey. By the time you reach Northwich, you have heard several more *nominies*, each one slightly different from the others.

What can it all mean? To find that out, we must travel further back in time and far away from here. We could wander through ancient Egypt at harvest time, or through any of the lands around the eastern Mediterranean, and hear nominies echoing over the hills in many languages. Greek travellers noted down these chants and compared them and they wrote about the impressive effect when heard from a distance. Nominies are probably as old as bread itself.

The great anthropologist Sir James Frazer, in *The Golden Bough,* studied many more recent versions from all over Europe and found a common thread running through them all. Our ancient ancestors, it seems, could not believe that corn came to ripeness by itself; such a miracle could only be the work of the *corn spirit.* This spirit lived amongst the crop and died at the end of the season (a hare's life-expectancy is not much better, incidentally). You could see, in the wavings and whisperings of the corn, where it went, fertilising each plant that it passed. Children were warned to keep away from the growing crop for fear of the spirit, sometimes personified as an ogre, or an old hag - a terrestrial sister of *Jinny Greenteeth*, perhaps. The cornfield was its only home so, as the reapers closed in, it skulked among the stalks that remained, along with the rabbits, hares, mice and other creatures. As the last stand of wheat fell, the spirit had no choice but to leap into the body of one of these animals and flee to an uncut field, while the reapers cobbed their sickles murderously. In other parts of Britain and Europe it might choose the form of a dog, cat, pig, wolf, goat, or even a human passer-by, but in mid- and north-east Cheshire it was the hare - a perfect fertility symbol, since the females can conceive while still pregnant. Each team of reapers raced to get its fields cut first and flush the hare (real or imaginary) into a neighbour's field. The laggard farmer who cut his corn last was a figure of fun - he was somehow lumbered with the old, spent corn spirit and his crops would not thrive next year. So far, so symbolic, but in ancient times this may have been much more literal. *Shutting* is Cheshire dialect for harvesting and there is evidence that, in those pagan days, a real hare used to be sacrificed - harvested along with the corn. The reapers would tie it up in the last stook, cut its throat with a sickle, then eat it at the harvest supper. By feasting on the body of the old corn spirit they ensured its rebirth the following year (is it coincidence that Cheshire farmers used to plough hares' skins into the ground when marl, dung, lime or other fertilisers were not to be had?). If we go back far enough, we find traces of human sacrifice - the charming details can be found in Frazer's work.

Harvest customs, until the late 19th century, were very varied and localised. Had we begun our imaginary journey from, say, Runcorn or Helsby, we would have heard different *nominies* and the harvesters would have called the procedure *cutting th' neck* rather than *shutting the hare.* While looking through some papers of the folklorist

147

Fletcher Moss, I came upon a letter which gives a first-hand description of the harvest rituals of Stretton, near Warrington. It was written by John Done, an elderly man who, in 1896, wrote down all the local folklore that he remembered from his youth: *"Cutting o'th Neck, was a great event in shearing time; and much extra work was gotten done by Masters keeping up the custom. I will tell the story as briefly as I can. Farmers would go around some eventide to see who was near to Cutting th'Neck and calculating upon their strength of hands and the breadth of land to shear over with their 'sickles' (only to be seen now hanging rusty in the Barns or else in Museums) and seeing that by a sprint they would probably be able to shout a neck first; it being listned for at the Farms arround; as to bands of reapers taking presidence – Well; the master would come into the wheatfield at the commencement of the day's work, and after 'stiding', how many Rods (corrupted into roods) were to be cut, and looking wise and calculating would say to the Leader, "What thinken ye George shall ye be able to cut th'neck to neet if ye try." Reply; "aye Mester with a little encouragement we shan." "A well then I'll go whom, and order a Supper of Roast Beef and pottatos, and Jacob Plumb Dumplings" (all of ripe black plumbs; no greensided ones) Made Rowley Powley; and when cut Oh, the delicious scent and flavour; makes my mouth water at the present day. When near the finish the master would select about 6 heads of wheat among the tallest straw; then clear the ground arround. Measure 10 or 12 paces off to stand and throw and the first to cut off the last ear wins (the prize being 1/–): the sickle being thrown in an horizontal manner pracktised by the reapers in the dinner hour: as soon as the neck is cut a tremendous shout of a, a, a Neck (several times) is raised: heard for more than a mile! After supper, over the Home Brewed (wholesome beverage that; not like the stuff now got from the Breweries), the usual Concert in which I have joined commencing with 'Colin and Phoebe' 'Highland Mary' 'Jockey to the Fair' 'The Garden Gate' &c. and sometimes finishing with a county dance.*

"Ah! Those happy times are now changed for ever!"

I know several retired farm workers who still recall the ancient rivalry among the harvest teams, but none now remembers the old customs. The combine harvester has banished both hares and people from the fields.

The Garden Gate

The day was gone, the moon shone bright the vill - age clock struck eight, Young Ma - ry 'hast - en'd with de - light un - to the gar - den gate. But what was there to make her sad? The gate was there but not the lad; Which made poor Ma - ry say and sigh "Was e - ver poor girl so used as I?"

Jockey to the Fair

'Twas on the morn of sweet May Day, When na - ture pain - ted all things gay, Taught birds to sing and lambs to play, And gilt the mead - ows fair; Young Jo - ckey, ear - ly in the morn, A - rose and tript it o'er the lawn; His Sun - day coat the youth put on, For Jen - ny had vow'd a - way to run With Jo - ckey to the fair, Jen - ry had vow'd a - way to run with Jo - ckey to the fair.

...the metallic mewing of peregrines as they wheel around the castle walls.

Chapter 26

The Kangaroos of Beeston Castle

Beeston Crag is an ancient place. The castle was built in 1225, and most people imagine that its history began in that far-distant year, when deer roamed the forests of Mondrem and Mara that stretched out for miles to the north. But no - centuries before that, the crag was topped by an Iron-Age hill fort and, before that, Bronze-Age people lived up here. And before that? Some say that ocean waves crashed against these rocks before the British Isles settled into their present shape. People have been coming here for centuries, too: some to make war (like the swashbuckling band of Royalists who scaled the cliff in 1642 and took the castle from the Roundheads), some to look for Richard II's legendary treasure (let me know if you find it) and others simply to nose around the ruins and enjoy the view. John Gerard paid at least one visit, for his *Historie of Plants* (1597) mentions wall pennywort, *"growing upon Bieston castle in Cheshire"*. Travellers going from London to Chester always found it an arresting and romantic sight; one coach passenger, in 1791, remarked that the crag *"together with some more blue distant mountains would make a perfect picture"*! But it was not until the late 19th century that Beeston became a regular place of pilgrimage. James Croston's book *Nooks and Corners of Lancashire and Cheshire* (1882) describes his own visit, with a vivid word-painting of the place as it was in his day. He got the train and wandered up from the former Beeston station, where *"a peaceful farmstead or two, surrounded by verdant pastures and fields of ripening corn, with here and there a cleanly whitewashed cottage, half hidden among the trees and hedges, are almost the only habitations we can see...A few minutes' walk along a sandy lane, that winds beneath the trees and across the sunbright meadows, where cattle are pasturing and haymakers are tossing the fragrant grass, brings us to the foot of the castle rock."*

Today, I've come to Beeston myself, with a copy of that book in my pocket, because I want to see what 120 years of upheaval have done to this landscape and its wildlife. Thanks to Dr. Beeching, I have had to pedal my way from Chester, but there's no better cycling country anywhere, particularly on a day such as this, with its warm sun, blue and white skies and soft showers blowing over from the west. Like Croston, I have come at hay-making time but, instead of a team of besmocked haymakers, I find just one tractor, towing a forage harvester to turn the grass into silage. After wandering up the half-wooded slopes, I come, at last, to the ruined gateway and, beyond that, the great spectacle of sky and land opens up. Now I can sit down, munch my bagging and survey the great open-air milk factory that we call the Cheshire Plain. Let's see how Croston described it: *"Glorious is the prospect that spreads around. What a wealth of pastoral loveliness lies before us, everywhere exhibiting the signs of fertility and cultivation. All within the limits is a green and beautiful expanse made up of copse and lea, of level meadow breadths and cattle-dappled pastures, that rejoice in the warm sunshine, with little hamlets and villages and shady lanes, old manor houses and churches - the monuments of the past mingling with the habitations of contemporary life and activity...The slumber of a summer day lies profoundly as a trance upon the scene. The lowing of the kine in the neighbouring meadows, the harsh note of the corncrake and the soft, dreamy call of the cuckoo are the only sounds that break upon the ear".*

Apart from those last two sounds, it's all reassuringly similar. Cattle still graze peacefully in the pastures as they have for the last 2,000 years or more. This is a view to be savoured slowly: a quilt of green and gold fields, punctured here and there by marl pits, framed by hedgerows and copses or broken up by wooded hills, all stretching to the horizon in every direction. No motorway or industrial estate intrudes and those horrid, noisy towns (where most of us choose to live) are pushed out towards the edges. But brick and tarmac are not the only enemies of this landscape. Through binoculars, I can see smudges in the fields where old pits have been filled in, and many of the hedges, on closer inspection, are disintegrating into rows of trees. And there are invisible changes too. How much fertiliser runs into those streams? How much of that summer haze is pollution?

Where are the clouds of butterflies and moths that used to fly out of the grass at haymaking time? How many water voles, hares, skylarks, peewits and barn owls still abide in these fields, woods and waters? Only a small fraction of the numbers that Croston might have seen. Every old person I spoke to in researching this book lamented the recent dwindling of those species and many others. My father used to say that, when cycling the Cheshire lanes in his youth, flocks of yellowhammers would weave in and out of the hedgerows, while coveys of grey partridges clattered up from each field as he passed. On my way here today, I failed to spot a single bird of either species. At one time, every farmer looked forward to the first of September, when he could go partridge-shooting, while the poachers made a tidy profit from netting them at night. There was even a time when Cheshire was credited with a partridge of its own. Latham's *General History of Birds* (1821) describes a handsome variety with russet underparts, which he calls the Cheshire Partridge (*Perdix montana*). It still turns up occasionally and is shown in some field guides, but Latham was mistaken in thinking them unique to Cheshire. Today, early grass-cutting leaves little cover for partridge chicks which, thanks to insecticides, often clem to death.

So, what *did* I see along the road to Beeston? I saw linnets (*brown* linnets, that is!), twittering on the telegraph wires and several charms of goldfinches (or *red* linnets) flew by. A century ago, bird-catchers had almost wiped both of those birds out. In Croston's day, only a few pairs of goldfinches still bred in Cheshire, although many of those whitewashed cottages that he described would have had a caged one beside the door. In those days, vast numbers were taken as nestlings or caught in nets as adults. Colonies of teasel sometimes mark the spots where bird-catchers once ticed them into their nets: on the banks of the Weaver at Northwich, for example, you may still see masses of teasel, descended from those planted by Bob Carden, the old ferryman, who loved to catch *nickers* in the early 20th century. The victims were sold cheaply in tiny cages and, if they survived, their owners would take them to certain pubs, called *Fancy Houses*, and enter them in singing competitions. Even as recently as 1937, Boyd was saying that *"in much of Cheshire it is still almost an event to see a nicker"*, but today they delight us almost everywhere.

Had I come via Delamere Forest, I might have seen other birds that have prospered well over the last century: nuthatches have colonised woods and parklands everywhere, goldcrests have multiplied in the conifer plantations and whatever we may think of the invasive rhododendron, it has boosted the numbers of one of our best songsters, the blackcap. A friend of mine,from Great Barrow showed me a pied flycatcher's nest in his garden recently - none had ever been known to nest in Cheshire when Croston was writing. And even here, sitting on the castle walls, there are compensations, for where he had the calls of the cuckoo and the corncrake to listen to, I have the guttural croak of the raven and the metallic mewing of peregrines as they wheel around the castle walls. Peregrines are no strangers to these parts, by the way - there is a 13th century record of the requisitioning of peregrine chicks from a Cheshire crag (Beeston or, perhaps, Helsby) for the King's own use.

Another cause for celebration is the great crested grebe. For Boyd, it was *the* Cheshire bird and, when the Cheshire Wildlife Trust was founded in 1962, it chose the grebe as its badge and had the bird's portrait drawn by the greatest of bird artists, Charles Tunnicliffe. But our county bird very nearly followed the bitterbump into obscurity. Thomas Pennant (1726-98) wrote: *"This species has been shot on Rosterne* [sic] *Mere in Cheshire; it is rather scarce in England...The underside of them, being dressed with the feathers on, are made into muffs and tippets; each bird sells for about fourteen shillings.* "The massacres went on and on until, by 1860, only about forty pairs were thought to remain in the whole of Great Britain - half of them in Cheshire, where many of the meres were attached to shooting estates, giving the birds some protection. JE Smith, in 1874, wrote that it was: *"now very scarce and will soon be extinct".* But the fashion for *grebe fur,* thankfully, died out before the grebe did and, from then on, it recolonised the rest of Britain from its ancient stronghold in Cheshire.

We can expect more success stories in the future because, in the 1990s, people began to rally round our wildlife as never before. The Cheshire Wildlife Trust teamed up with a variety of other organisations to produce the *Countdown Programme*: a set of Species Recovery Plans for many of the beleaguered creatures that I have lamented in earlier chapters of this book, including the peewit, grey partridge, spotted flycatcher, nightjar, barn owl, brown hare, otter, polecat, great crested newt, adder, slow worm - and many of the less popular creepy or slimy ones - beetles, spiders and snails. Not only that, several species that have not been seen for many years have been physically brought back. Take butterflies, for example. When Croston stood here in 1882, the silver-studded blue was found on heathlands all the way from Alderley Edge to Bidston Hill but, by 1925, they had all gone. Yet, if you go along to Thurstaston Common in July, you will see a thriving colony - they were reintroduced there in 1994. In 1882, the sand dunes along the Wirral coast were enlivened by natterjack toads, as well. Children called them *jar-bobs,* perhaps because their trilling croak sounds like nightjar song, but eventually, thanks to an explosion of housing and golf links, they too became extinct. In 1996, 7,500 tadpoles were collected from the Lancashire coast (where they have a better name for natterjacks: *Southport nightingales*) and released near Hoylake. Within a few years, a new generation of adults was running about on the dunes as of yore.

1996 was also the Year of the Dormouse! In that year, a carefully-chosen Cheshire wood was filled with nestboxes and 29 precious, captive-bred dormice were released into it. Would they survive...? In the Middle Ages, there would have been no problem, for Cheshire had plenty of coppice woodlands, where timber and underwood were grown for all life's necessities, not to mention all those famous *magpie* houses. Such woods were open, airy places which, in spring, were awash with flowers and rang with the songs of nightingales. They had a rich shrub-layer of elder, bramble, hazel, hawthorn and honeysuckle where, in the back-end, dormice could pig out on nuts and berries before hibernation. But, as we can see clearly from up here, the coppice woods are long gone and cows now rule this land. The isolated game coverts of the plain are another type of wood altogether: close-canopied and dark, without the tangled scrub that dormice need. By 1900, there were none left in the county. But the Class of '96 did survive, and many produced young in their first year. The latest news is that the dormice have gone forth and multiplied, spreading into other woods, far from their first home.

In 2002, it was the turn of harvest mice. The sparse records of the last 200 years suggest that they have always been rare in Cheshire, but their scientific name, *Micromys minutus*, reminds us that they are easily overlooked! So when, in 1997, a nest was found at Aston, near Nantwich, people began to search for harvest mice in earnest. Nests were soon found in a few more places, but it was clear that the species needed a leg-up. Again, a suitable site was chosen - no, not a cornfield, but a network of reedy ditches and bramble-strangled hedges - and captive-bred mice were set free. This time, however, hundreds of mice were needed, so volunteers took breeding pairs home with them and, before long, they were rolling off the production line.

Projects like these bring *touchy-feely* fun into wildlife conservation and, so long as we remember that harvest mice are not pets, they restore a little of the day-to-day contact that was the birthright of our ancestors. In fact, researching this book has convinced me that people and wild creatures need each other: we both thrive better when our lives are intertwined. Separate us and we both suffer, like Croston's haymakers who left the land around the same time as the corncrakes and for much the same reason. Our not-so-distant ancestors were involved with wild creatures every day of their lives, from the curing of their first bout of whooping cough or bed-wetting until their deaths were announced to the bees. I am not suggesting that we return to those practices or, for that matter, that we should swallow spiders or incarcerate live shrews in trees, but I do think there is more to experiencing wildlife than watching birds through binoculars. I also suspect that a child who is free to snig for eels and fry moorhens' eggs over an open fire will be more passionate about conservation than one who has merely been dragged along to supervised pond-dips. That's one reason why, I think, the folk-history of wildlife should be remembered. Another is the fact that, to conserve birds and animals, we must know them thoroughly. And who knows them best? Those who see them every day: the farm labourers and poachers that Boyd learned from, the shepherds and wildfowlers that Coward consulted, the fishermen that taught Ellison so much, and the old farmers and gamekeepers that I have chatted to myself. Even the folklore and superstition is not a complete irrelevance, for it is our last link with the myths of our very distant ancestors - thoroughly amoral people who hunted for their very lives, alongside wolves, lynx and bears. Sometimes even conservationists need to be reminded that we are animals ourselves and were once wild like them.

I could spend all day gazing on this countryside. What will become of it, do you think? If the population goes on multiplying it may, one day, be a sea of neo-Georgian estates and our grandchildren shall have only urban wildlife for company. On the other hand, if the polar ice-caps melt, the real sea will pour in and this crag will be like Hilbre Island at high tide, but crammed with squabbling people instead of birds. But the farmer has finished cutting his hay now and the shadows of the hedgerow trees lie long across the fields, telling me to begin the ride home, so, like many before me, I say a silent prayer for the future of Cheshire, its cuckoo trees, its ancient rookeries, its slowly-returning otters, its debatable smelt, its few remaining dialect-speakers, its dimly-remembered folklore and all its undiscovered history before making my way down to the flowery walls of the castle's outer ward. Over the centuries, nature has softened the edges of this warlike place, so that the crumbling masonry now looks like a rock garden, colonised by wallflowers, herb-Robert and - aha! - wall pennywort just as Gerard promised over 400 years ago. In Croston's time, sheep and deer grazed on these slopes: *"Brushwood and*

*bracken and the wild, old, wandering bramble border the way; and now and then a
timid sheep rushes out from some shady nook and gazes wonderingly at us as we go by.
The turf in places is short and slippery, for the rabbits keep it closely cropped...A pair of
kangaroos are disporting themselves among the moss-grown fragments, and a few deer
are quietly browsing upon the green turf; but there is..."*

Hang on. What was that about *kangaroos*? Must go and do some more research!

The End

Bibliography

Bickerton, L., Memories of a Cheshire Childhood (1996).
Birch Reynardson, T.S., Sports and Anecdotes of Bygone Days (1887).
Boyd, A.W., A Country Parish (1951), Country Diary of a Cheshire Man (1946).
Bridge, J., Old Cheshire Proverbs (1917).
Brockholes, J.F., The Birds of Wirral (1874).
Cheshire Notes and Queries.
Cheshire Sheaf, The.
Chester Chronicle, The.
Coward, T.A., Bird Haunts and Nature Memories (1922), Picturesque Cheshire (1903).
Coward T.A. and Oldham C., Invertebrate Fauna of Cheshire (1910).
Croston, J., Nooks and Corners of Lancashire and Cheshire (1882).
Darlington, T., Folk-speech of South Cheshire (1887).
Dodgson, Place-names of Cheshire (1970-1997).
Egerton Leigh, Lt. Col., Ballads and Legends of Cheshire (1867), Glossary of Words used in the Dialect of Cheshire (1877).
Egerton-Warburton, G., In a Cheshire Garden (1912).
Ellison, N., The Wirral Peninsular (1955).
Farrar, G., Feathered Folk of an Estuary (1938).
Frazer, Sir J., The Golden Bough (1890-1915).
Gamlin, H., Twixt Mersey and Dee (1897).
Gentleman's Magazine, The (1742).
Gerard, J., The Historie of Plants (1597).
Heaton, A. Duck Decoys (2001).
King, D., The Vale Royal of England (1656).
Leigh, C., The Natural History of Lancashire, Cheshire and the Peak in Derbyshire, etc. (1700).
Leland, J., Itinerary, (1535-43).
Lucas, H.V., Homage to Cheshire (1939-60).
Lupton, A Thousand Notable Things of Sundry Sortes, etc., (1595).
Macclesfield Courier, The.
Manchester City news, The.
Marriott, P.J., Red Sky at Night, Shepherd's Delight?
Moss, F., Chronicles of Cheadle (1894), Folklore (1898), Pilgrimages to Old Homes (1913).
Neilson, H.B., Auld Lang Syne (1935).
Palmer, M. (Ed.), Plants, People, Places (Newsletters 7 & 8, 1995-6).
Sainter, J.D., Scientific Rambles around Macclesfield (1878).
Stockport Advertiser, The.
Topsell, R., The History of Four-footed Beasts (1607).
Tunnicliffe, C.F., My Country Book (1942).
Tunstall, B., The Shiny Night (1931).
Warburton, R.E. Egerton, Hunting Songs, 6th edition (1877).
White, G., The Natural History of Selbourne (1776).

Index of Species and Glossary

(Numbers refer to chapters. Bold print = main references)

Dove, Stock 8, 15, 24
Dragonflies **7**
Ducks 3, 11, 24
Duck, Mandarin **8**
Duck, Ruddy **8**
Duck, Tufted **8**
Dumberdash - A downpour
Dunlin 9, 19
Dunna - Don't
Dunnock 1, 24
Eagle, Golden 4
Eagle, White-tailed 18
Earthworms 5
Eel, Common 5, **11**, 16, 24
Eel, Conger 9
Fey - to remove topsoil
Fieldfare **1**, 24
Flit - To move house
Flounder **9, 11**
Flusker - To fly in a confused way, as newly-fledged birds do
Flycatcher, Pied 26
Flycatcher, Spotted **21**
Fox 4, **6**, 9, 11, 24
Frem folk - Strangers
Fricken - To frighten
Frog, Common **3, 5, 7**, 22
Gadfly 24
Gannet 18
Gawm out - To work out
Gen - Given
Gnats 3
Godwits 9
Goldfinch **24, 26**
Gollop - to swallow greedily
Goose, Barnacle **19, 22**
Goose, Canada **8, 11**, 19
Goose, Pinkfoot **19**
Goshawk
Grebe, Black-necked **8**
Grebe, Great Crested **26**
Greenfinch 20, 21, 24
Grouse, Black **2**, 18
Gull, Black-headed **3**, **11**, 20,24
Gull, Greater Black-backed 9
Gull, Herring 9
Gull, Lesser Black-backed 3
Hamster, Golden 8

Han - have
Harbouration - Place to stay
Hare, Belgian **9**
Hare, Brown 4, 5, **6**, 9, **25**
Hare, Mountain **8**
Hawfinch 20
Heckle-tempered - touchy
Hedgehog **5**, 9, **11**, **20**, 24
Heron, Grey 24
Heron, Night **7**
Herring 9
Hippopotamus 4
Howd - hold
Jackdaw 15, **20**, 22
Jay 15, **20**
Jed - dead
Jingal - a type of musket once used in India and China
Jinny Greenteeth - a water-hag, invented to scare children away from water
Junco, Dark-eyed 18
Kangaroo 26
Kestrel 24
Kine - Cows
Kite, Red **2**, **20**
Kittlen - to have kittens
Knot 9, 19
Lamprey **11**
Lap - to wrap
Lapwing (see peewit)
Linnet 9, 24, 26
Lizard **7**
Loach, Stone **11**
Lozzack - to laze, loaf
Lugworm 9
Lynx 4
Magpie 15, **17**, **20,** 22, 24
Mallard 19
Marrow - Partner, mate
Marten, Pine **2**, 4, 15
Martin, House **21**
Maxonian - a native of Macclesfield
Mell supper - harvest supper
Midges 3
Mink **8**
Mither - a nuisance
Mixen - a dung heap
Mizzicky - boggy, marshy

Mole **3**, **20**
Mon - man
Moorhen **11**, 18, 24
Moths 18
Mouse, Harvest **26**
Mouse, House 3, **5**, 9, 11
Mouse, Wood 9
Mullet 11
Mun - must
Neest - nest
Neezle - to nestle
Nesh - soft, sensitive
Newt, Great Crested **7**, 24
Newt, Smooth **7**, 24
Nightingale **10**, 18
Nightjar **2**, **22**, **24**
Nutcracker 18
Nuthatch 26
Octopus 9
Otter **2**, 4, 8, **20**
'Owd - hold
Owl, Barn 18, **20**, **22**
Owl, Little **8**
Owl, Tawny 3, **24**
Oyster-catcher 9, 19
Partridge, Grey 18, 20, **26**
Peewit **3**, **11**, **24**
Perch 16
Peregrine 15, **26**
Petrel, Kermadec 18
Pheasant 20
Pigeon, Feral 15, **21**
Pigeon, Wood 3, 8, **15**, 24
Pike **16**
Pintail 18, 19, 23
Pintle - penis
Pipefish **9**
Pipit, Meadow 1, 9, 24
Plat - bridge
Plover, Golden **22**, **24**
Plover, Grey 24
Plover, Ringed 9
Plover, Little Ringed 8
Pochard 8
Polecat **2**, 15,20
Porpoise, Harbour 9, **12**
Posset - a remedy for colds made with hot milk curdled with beer, wine, spices, etc.

Quail, Common **10**
Rabbit 5, **9**, 11, **24**
Rackussing - noisy
Rat, Brown 9, 11, 13, **20**, 24
Raven **10**, 20, **22**, 26
Redpoll **24**
Redshank 9, **11**
Redwing 24
Reen - rain
Reest - Rest
Rhinoceros 4
Roach 16
Robin 3, **21**
Rockling 9
Rod - 1 rod = 5 ½ yards
Rompetty - restive, nervous
Rood - 4 roods = 1 acre
Rook 3, 11, **14**, 22
Rubbitch - rubbish
Salmon 5, 9, 11, 19
Sandgrouse, Pallas's **10**, 18
Scutter - to scramble away
Sea-anemone 9
Seal, Common 9
Seal, Grey **9**
Sea-scorpion 9
Seck - sack
Seethe - to boil
Seine - a fishing net with weights and floats, usually hauled ashore
Shag 18
Shan - shall
Shark, Basking **12**
Shattery - hare-brained
Shelduck 9, 19
Shippon - Cow-shed
Shoveler 19, 23
Shrews **13**
Shrimps 9
Shuttance (to get) - to get rid of
Sich - Such
Siskin 24
Sken - to squint
Skittering - scattering
Skrike - to cry out
Skrike of day - cock-crow
Skylark 3, 9
Slat - to dump down roughly

159

The author is interested in any comments you may have on this book, particularly if it jogs any memories of your own.

You will find a page on the Cheshire Wildlife Trust website (www.wildlifetrust.org.uk/cheshire) where you can also learn more about the work of the Trust. Alternatively you can write to the author via the publisher.

Erratum: Rear cover, Postheme Mere
should be Rostherne Mere.